they
dared
to dream

# THOMAS A. FRY, JR.

# they
# dared
# to dream

WORD BOOKS, Publisher
Waco, Texas

THEY DARED TO DREAM

Library of Congress Catalog Card No.: 72-188061
Printed in the United States of America.

For permission to include quotations from copyrighted material, the
following acknowledgments are gratefully made:

*I Have a Dream,* by Martin Luther King, Jr. Reprinted by permission
of Joan Daves. Copyright © 1963 by Martin Luther King, Jr.

From "Pater Patriae as Pater Familias," by Frederic Fox. © Copyright 1963 by American Heritage Publishing Co., Inc. Reprinted by
permission from *American Heritage* Magazine.

From *God in the White House* by Edmund Fuller and David E. Green.
© 1968 by Edmund Fuller and David Eliot Green. Used by permission
of Crown Publishers, Inc.

Adapted from *The World Book Year Book* © 1964 Field Enterprises
Educational Corporation.

From *Alone* by Richard E. Byrd. Copyright 1938 by Richard E. Byrd;
renewed © 1966 by Marie A. Byrd. Reprinted by permission of G. P.
Putnam's Sons.

From *Markings,* by Dag Hammarskjöld, trans. by Leif Sjöberg and
W. H. Auden. Copyright © 1964 by Alfred A. Knopf, Inc. and Faber
and Faber, Ltd. Reprinted by permission of Alfred A. Knopf, Inc.

From *The Life of Woodrow Wilson* by Josephus Daniels. Used by permission of Reprint House International.

Scripture quotations marked RSV are from the Revised Standard
Version of the Bible, copyright 1946 and 1952 by the Division of
Christian Education of the National Council of the Churches of Christ
in the United States of America. Used by permission.

*Louise and I dedicate this book to*
*our living parents*
*Mr. and Mrs. C. W. Sullivan*
*and*
*Mrs. Thomas A. Fry*
*who have been our heroes*

*and*

*to our lively grandson, Thomas A. Fry, IV*
*with whom we would share these dreams*

# Contents

# Preface

Since my childhood days I have been interested in and inspired by the lives of great men. Shortly after I learned to read, my mother saw to it that an interesting story of the life of some hero was always on the table by my bed. I still remember the thrill of reading about David Livingstone, Borden of Yale, Adoniram Judson, "Stonewall" Jackson, Robert E. Lee, Oliver Cromwell, and Richard the Lion-Hearted.

Because these men made such profound impressions on me, it occurred to me that I should ask myself the question as to why people who lived after Jesus should not be better than people who lived before him. If Jesus does save us from our sin, should not those who live after him be more free from sin than those who came before? If the Holy Spirit has any power in the lives of men, should not men after Pentecost lead more effective lives than the men who lived before Pentecost?

With this background I have written these chapters, telling of men of more recent times whose names we know and respect who could serve as inspiration to us now, as Adoniram Judson was to me as a child. I am well aware that facets in these men's lives exist that are embarrassing to their friends, but not nearly such serious embarrassment as the obvious failures of Abraham and David. It has been my desire to glean from these lives those special qualities which would be worthy examples to us.

The following chapters are not meant to be definitive biographies. I have sought to say that men have lived who stood for moral and ethical principles and who were even willing to die for them.

These studies have proved invaluable to me and have made a better man of me. I hope that they will be helpful to you who read them.

I owe a great debt of gratitude to students whose biographies are quoted, to my mother who first started my reading biographies, to the congregation that has found this a helpful form of preaching, to the friends whose criticism has forced me to change many of my ideas, and to my secretary, Dorothy Headrick, who has typed and retyped my manuscript.

# Thomas More

# A Man for All Seasons

INTEREST IN SIR THOMAS MORE has been revived in recent years by a great play and a magnificent movie entitled *A Man for All Seasons*. More has been in the news again as officials of the British government have tried but failed to secure a pardon for him. More's book *Utopia* still ranks with Augustine's *City of God* and Plato's *Republic* as being one of the noblest visions of the future possibility of men that ever entered the heart of man. This vision is still studied by those who dream of better things.

These facts would not be enough to warrant the consideration of Sir Thomas More in a chapter having as a theme, "Of whom the world was not worthy," were it not for the fact that certain personal qualities in this man's life have distinguished him from a majority of people who lived during his time. If you would study the heroes mentioned in the eleventh chapter of Hebrews about whom the author of that book says, "The world was not worthy," then surely you would rank Sir Thomas More morally and spiritually as a giant. To even put Rahab, a harlot, in the same classification as More indicates lack of moral and spiritual discernment. Certainly "Of whom the world was not worthy" must be said of him if it can be said of those listed in the eleventh chapter of Hebrews.

Thomas More was born February 7, 1478, and was executed in the summer of 1535. He entered Oxford University in 1492, the year Columbus discovered America. For four years during his twenties he wavered between giving his life to the church and going into law practice. During these four years he observed the strict discipline of a monastic order. Finally deciding that his life vocation should be in the law profession rather than in the church, he left the monastic order, even though until his death he continued many of the disciplines of that order. When he was twenty-seven years old, he married. He very quickly rose in prominence in the legal and political professions. He earned the enmity of King Henry VII, but after Henry's death More became the close friend of Henry VIII. For years More was so close to Henry VIII that the king would come to his home for discussions of history and astronomy. Henry VIII consumed more of Sir Thomas' time than More thought it wise. Finally he was made Lord Chancellor of England, the highest political and judicial post available. This was only after he had been Speaker of the House of Commons. He broke with Henry VIII over Henry's proposed divorce of the queen and his desire to marry Anne Boleyn. One of the focal points of the discussion was whether or not the pope had authority over the king. On the technical grounds that Thomas More accepted the authority of the church and the pope in the case of the divorce and remarriage, Henry VIII ordered him tried and executed. This was done in 1535.

Throughout history public figures have grown wealthy by capitalizing on the opportunities that have come through their political jobs. I heard not long ago of a politician who owned a house worth over $50,000 and who had stocks and bonds worth over a quarter of a million dollars. During his political career he had never made over $15,000 a year. When questioned by one of our courts as to how he had accumulated so much, he said that his wife had saved dimes and quarters and that she had been a good manager. Quite obviously a man cannot save a quarter of a million dollars on a $15,000 salary just because his wife saves dimes and quarters and is a good manager.

Thomas More did not allow himself to become wealthy. It was the custom in those days for a family to make a gift to a judge after he had rendered a verdict in their favor. A Mr. Vaughan received such a verdict from Sir Thomas More, and at the next appropriate occasion his wife brought to More a very valuable golden goblet. More refused the goblet. He saw he was offending the lady by his refusal, and so he finally accepted. He had his servant bring in wine, filled the goblet and drank a toast to Mr. Vaughan. After his toast he told Mrs. Vaughan that now that the goblet was his he could do with it what he chose, and the thing that he wanted to do more than anything else was to give the goblet to her husband, which he did.

On another occasion he felt impelled to accept a gift, and so he sent to the donor something far more valuable than he had received.

As we look at contemporary society and see an accumulation of wealth in businessmen and politicians who have lived far beyond their salaries and yet accumulated much of this world's goods, it would be a refreshing thing to see them return to the integrity and idealism of this man who would not use his office for personal gain. When a man rises above selfishness to accept public responsibility, it is a thing worthy of note in our society. It is partly on this ground that I would say that Sir Thomas More was a man "Of whom the world was not worthy."

His personal integrity was further evidenced by a case that he tried involving one of his sons-in-law. Knowing that judges looked after their own families, the new son-in-law thought he had every right to expect More to return a verdict in his favor. He and the entire court were shocked when More ruled against his son-in-law. When asked about his decision against his son-in-law, More said, "Were . . . my father on one side and the devil on the other side (his cause being good) the devil should have right." When one sees the nepotism in politics and business, this comes as a refreshing wind. When we observe the number of fathers who expect their sons' traffic tickets to be fixed or who try to get their sons out of scrapes with the law, or when we see justice bent to favor particular families or individuals, we see a crying need for public figures whose moral and spiritual lives prevent them from using political position in favor of their friends and family. If Samson, with his misuse of power and weakness toward being manipulated, belongs in the list of men "Of whom the world was not worthy," then surely Thomas More belongs there. How we need men today who will be transformed by the Christian gospel as More was transformed.

In studying the life of Sir Thomas More I was struck by his sensitivity to the people with whom he dealt. A vivid illustration of this took place at the time of his execution. His executioner, a public official paid to carry out the orders of execution, was

very hesitant about beheading a man like Thomas More. More
sensed his feeling of guilt. To show this man he had nothing
against him, More gave him a gift prior to the execution. When
on the gallows the man hesitated, More said to him, "Pluck up
thy spirits, man, and be not afraid to do thine office." This is in
sharp contrast to the man who gets angry at the policeman who
has stopped him, or at the clerk who is carrying out the policies
of the store, or at the representative of the bank who is trying
to do his job.

I was at the airport the other day. A man was protesting to
the clerk over the fact that he was trying to charge him for
extra luggage. The clerk had rules and regulations which he
was trying to follow. So many times we expect people who are
doing their jobs to bend the rules for us, but Thomas More was
a man who respected those who were doing their jobs and he
was sensitive to their embarrassment.

His extreme sensitivity extended to another area. The story of
Jacob and Rachel reveals the dilemma of Thomas More. Jacob
loved Rachel and wanted to marry her. Her father, Laban, told
him he would have to work seven years for him before he would
allow them to be married. Jacob did this and the marriage took
place. To Jacob's amazement, Laban substituted the other daughter, Leah, for Rachel. When Jacob complained, Laban told him
it was not proper to have a younger daughter marry before an
older one. If he wanted to marry Rachel he would have to
marry Leah first and then work seven more years for Rachel.
This he did. This idea of marrying the older daughter prevailed
down through the time of Shakespeare. You recall the incident
in the *Taming of the Shrew* when the father would not allow
the younger daughter to marry until the older daughter was
married.

Thomas More fell in love with the second daughter in a family
of three girls. Realizing the embarrassment this would cause the
older daughter, he proposed to her and married her instead. I
realize this raises many questions in your mind, but no matter
what the question you cannot help but admire this man's sensitivity to persons.

We are living in a day when if a man marries and then finds
someone he thinks is more attractive, he is inclined to divorce
his wife. But Thomas More controlled his love life to the extent

that he put the personal needs of others before his own affection.

When you look at the life of David who murdered Uriah to marry Uriah's wife, Bathsheba, is it any wonder that I would suggest Thomas More as being one "Of whom the world was not worthy?"

When More was faced with the knowledge that he would have to resign as Lord Chancellor of England, or agree to Henry VIII's divorce and marriage to Anne Boleyn, he faced a tremendous financial problem. His income would be cut to no more than ten percent of what it had been.

How does a man face the challenge of such a cut in his income? Most men would say that they would have to compromise their moral standards to maintain their living standards. Instead, More called in his family and told them that they would have to let their home go and move to much cheaper accommodations. He suggested that they move first into one area. If this was above their budget after the first year, they would move to a cheaper locale. If this also proved to be above the budget, they would then make another move into an area that was considered a slum area.

As I look about me and see the number of people who have compromised their moral standards to maintain their living standards, this is a refreshing breeze. I see men who say that they have to make a living; therefore, they have to do some things they think are not quite right. Others say that they cannot get a job if they express their convictions in their community. In both cases they are saying living standards are more important than moral standards.

The final issue in Thomas More's life was whether or not he would put the king above his church and his faith. If he would agree to the supremacy of the king above the spiritual order he would save his life. In our own day we have this same conflict —will we obey the state, or will we obey our conscience? This left Thomas More in a very vulnerable position, for there are always hundreds of people who will compromise their conscience to the government. In taking a stand against public opinion, you are faced with the charge of being arrogant. Who was Sir Thomas More to stand against the cardinal and the bishops of the church? Would they not know more of the Bible and religion than he did? Who was he to stand against Henry VIII? He acknowledged this difficulty and told them if they would but prove him wrong from the Bible, he would sign the necessary documents. They were not able to prove him wrong. They continued in their compromise. He continued to death in his conviction. It has never been popular to stand against the state, even in the name of Jesus Christ.

Because this man put the kingdom of God and his righteousness above all other kingdoms and all other values, it can be said of him that he was one "Of whom the world was not worthy."

Earlier I mentioned that Thomas More wrote the book *Utopia*. He had previously been a lecturer dealing with Augustine's *City of God*. A large part of his life was given to trying to find the ideal social and political arrangements under which man might live.

His study of Plato's *Republic* and Augustine's *City of God* and his careful observation of the world around him led him to write *Utopia*. His vision was based upon insights of those who had gone before him and upon his knowledge of the world about him.

How many of you have read *Utopia*? How many have read *City of God*? Let me ask you another question. How many of you have watched "Guiding Light" or "As the World Turns," professional football games or ice hockey games? How many paperbacks dealing with salacious love or violent murder have you read? Have you read any of James Bond or Erle Stanley Gardner or Eric Segal's *Love Story*? If you have time to watch any of these television shows, or read any of these books, can you honestly say that you have not had time to read *Utopia* or *The Vietnam Reader*, or books by Dietrich Bonhoeffer or Karl Menninger?

Should not our reading time also be committed to our mental, moral, and spiritual growth? Thomas More prepared himself, developed his vision, and then committed himself to a political job through which he sought to make his values a reality in the world.

These values of Thomas More, as expressed in his writings, are not all of the same high moral standard that we would support, but as far back as the fifteenth century this man was advocating universal education at government expense, and he also advocated jobs for everyone. He sought for a community where there could be many churches that would accept each other. Here was a man with vision far beyond his time, and it came from his commitment to Jesus Christ, his study of the Scriptures, his familiarity with the great ideas of history.

Perhaps one of the reasons our world has advanced no farther in the moral sphere is that we spend too much time watching "Guiding Light" and too little time reading about the Light of the world.

When I look at this man's vision and contrast it with the vision of Barak about whom it was said, "Of whom the world was not worthy," I am sure that this text ought to be applied to Thomas More. I would like very much to think that you and I had enriched our own vision and applied ourselves to the implication of that vision that it could also be said to us, "Of whom the world [is] not worthy."

It was More's habit on Friday to devote himself to prayer and "spiritual exercise." He gave careful instruction to his children. He made one statement so regularly that they memorized it and were able to repeat it. "It is now no mastery for you children to go to heaven. For everybody giveth you good example. You see virtue rewarded and vice punished, so that you are carried up to heaven even by the chins. But if you live in the time that no man will give you good counsel, nor no man give you good example, when you shall see virtue punished, and vice rewarded, if you will then stand fast, and firmly stick to God upon pain of life, if you be but half good, God will allow you for whole good. . . . We may not look at our pleasure to go to heaven in feather beds, it is not that way. For our Lord himself went thither with great pain, and by many tribulations, which is the path wherein he walked thither, and the servant may not look to be in better case than his master." Note that he says that they have seen in him a good example. He felt that the father's responsibility to his children was to set a good example to them.

In his book *The Naked Ape* Desmond Morris indicates that we create real problems for our children when what we say is at variance with our own inner life. "If the mother is making tense and agitated movements, no matter how concealed, she will communicate these to her child. If at the same time she gives a strong smile, it does not fool the infant, it only confuses it. Two conflicting messages are being transmitted. If this is done a great deal it may be permanently damaging and cause the child serious difficulties when making social contacts and adjustments later in life." [1]

A unique thing about Thomas More was the way he tied together his teachings and his example. Obviously the Holy Spirit caused this man to rise above the common herd of man. "His children rise up and call him blessed." "May his tribe increase."

A foundation stone of Thomas More's life was his belief that once a person is created within the womb, he then lives eternally. He firmly believed that we must answer to God for deeds done in the flesh and must give account for every action and attitude performed during this life. We must all stand before the judgment seat of God. From this belief came the conclusion voiced earlier by Paul that the "sufferings of this present time are not worthy to be compared to the glories that shall be revealed in us."

It was this belief in eternal life that was partially responsible for the sterling qualities of character and commitment that we have seen in Thomas More. It was this belief in eternal life that enabled him to face the executioner without fear or dread. Belief in eternal life becomes a guiding star in current events and a source of hope for future destiny.

In the recent play about the life of Sir Thomas More, the author was trying to say that in the springtime of life Thomas More could be an inspiration, that in the summertime of life he could be a comfort, that in the fall and winter he was a man who brought hope. He was a man for all seasons "Of whom the world was not worthy."

It has not been my interest to bring you information about Sir Thomas More so much as it is my goal to show you that such a life can be lived and to so inspire you that you will seek to live as adequately and gloriously in this generation as Thomas More lived in his.

# George Washington

# Father of His Country

Have you ever tried to crack a pecan between your fingers? I am not suggesting cracking a pecan by pressing two pecans together, but just by pressing a pecan between two fingers. It is extremely difficult. I was interested in watching the movie on Williamsburg which portrayed George Washington as cracking a black walnut between his fingers.

George Washington was a man of physical strength, character, and leadership. Henry Lee said of him, "First in war. First in peace. First in the hearts of his countrymen."

George Washington was a man like as we are. He had problems just as we have problems.

Many of you men can sympathize with him. He had financial problems. The American Revolution and the expense of running his household had left him with many debts. When he was told that he was to be elected president of the United States, he felt that he must put his family and financial affairs in order. This would necessitate the borrowing of substantial sums of money.

He finally decided he would have to raise over one thousand pounds, but his credit was not good enough. Businessmen were not willing to lend him the money. Finally, he turned to Charles Carroll, "most monied man I was acquainted with," but Carroll, a signer of the Declaration of Independence, also refused. He was finally able to borrow five hundred pounds from Richard Conway of Alexandria at a rate of 6 percent. This paid his most pressing debts and left him nothing. "He had to beg another hundred pounds so that he could pay his expenses to New York and the Presidency." [1]

19

We are often prone to judge a man by his wealth and to be very critical of a man who has to borrow money to pay personal expenses. I do not think that it lessens George Washington's contribution to American history to realize that like many of us he had serious financial problems.

Washington had no children of his own. Martha, his wife, had two children by a previous marriage. She was an indulgent, fearful mother. When Washington finally sent Jackie Custis off to school, he said, "I hope that the school will be able to make him fit for more useful purposes than a horse racer." At that time Jackie's only interests were dogs, horses, and guns.[2] The headmaster said of him: "I must confess to you I never did in my life know a youth so exceedingly indolent or so surprisingly voluptuous: One would suppose Nature had intended him for some Asiatic Prince." [3]

In addition to Martha's two children, there were nieces, nephews, and grandchildren. His letters sound like the ones we write our children. To one of his nephews he wrote:

"Dear George: . . . The first and great object with you at present is to acquire, by industry, and application such knowledge as your situation enables you to obtain, as will be useful to you in life. . . . I do not mean by a close application to your studies that you should not enter into those amusements which are suited to your age and station; they can be made to go hand in hand with each other, and, used in their proper seasons, will ever be found to be a mutual assistance to one another. . . . One thing, however, I would strongly impress upon you, viz., that when you have leisure to go into company that it should always be of the best kind that the place you are in will afford; by this means you will constantly be improving your manners and cultivating your mind while you are relaxing from your books; and good company will always be found much less expensive than the bad. . . . I cannot enjoin too strongly upon you a due observance of economy and frugality, as you well know yourself, the present state of your property and finances will not admit of any unnecessary expense. The article of clothing is now one of the chief expenses you will incur, and in this, I fear, you are not so economical as you should be. Decency and cleanliness will always be the first object in the dress of a judicious and sensible man; a conformity to the prevailing fashion in a certain degree is necessary; but it does not from thence follow that a man should always get a new coat, or other clothes, upon every trifling change in the mode, when perhaps he has two or three very good ones by him. A person who is anxious to be a leader of the fashion, or one of the first to follow it will certainly appear in the eyes of judicious men, to have nothing better than a frequent change of dress to recommend him to notice. . . . Should you or Lawrence therefore behave in such manner as to occasion any complaint being made to me, you may depend upon losing that place which you now have in my affections, and any future hopes you may have from me. But if, on the contrary, your conduct is such as to merit my regard, you may always depend upon the warmest attachment, and sincere affection of your Friend and Uncle. /s/ G. Washington" [4]

Douglas Southall Freeman, the great biographer of George Washington, concluded that as a parent he was "a failure." [5] Many great men and women have been failures as parents. Our present social conscience makes failure as a parent the number one failure of life. I have heard people say that Franklin Roosevelt had no right to be president because they judged him a failure as a father. Would it not be a shame to set this up as the one absolute standard and thus leave the George Washingtons out of positions of leadership?

Washington was not always liked, nor was he always successful. He was made commander-in-chief of the Revolutionary Army, as a compromise between the southern and northern colonies. He did not always prove to be a good general and made many serious mistakes—one at New York almost lost the Revolutionary War.

There was intrigue among his officers. At one time the intrigue was so serious that a group of the leaders in the Continental Congress sided with some of Washington's subordinates in an effort to oust him.

As president he achieved many things during his first administration, but like so many of our presidents his second administration ran into serious trouble with Congress and with his cabinet.

A Philadelphia newspaper, published by Ben Franklin's son-in-law, ran an article in 1796 while Washington was still president saying, "If ever a nation was deceived by a man, the American nation has been deceived by Washington." [6]

It was Thomas Paine, the great patriot, who wrote, "And as to you, sir, treacherous in private friendship . . . and a hypocrite in public life, the world will be puzzled to decide whether you are an apostate or an imposter, whether you have abandoned good principles, or whether you ever had any." [7]

If you think you are discouraged, read Thomas Jefferson's discussion of a cabinet meeting on August 2, 1793. "The president was much inflamed, got into one of those passions when he cannot command himself, ran on much on the personal abuse which had been bestowed on him, defied any man on earth to produce one single act of his since he had been in the government which was not done on the purest motives . . . that by God he had rather be in his grave than in his present situation. That he had rather be on his farm than to be made emperor of the world and yet they are charging him with wanting to be king. . . ." [8]

George Washington had other things against him. He was a disadvantaged child. His father died when he was eleven, and he was brought up by his half-brother, Lawrence. In a day when boys like John Adams went to Harvard, George had little or no formal schooling. His letters indicate an inability to spell. As a young man, he had smallpox, which left his face badly marked. As a middle-aged man he lost his teeth and had very ill fitting false teeth for the rest of his life, marring his appearance and his ability to eat.

George Washington was not able to win the girls that he wanted to marry. In his first two attempts at marriage, he was turned down flatly. He then fell in love with a lady who was not available, and then on the fourth try he succeeded in winning the hand of the widow, Martha Custis.

In spite of all of these difficulties Washington deserves the title of father of his country. He served as general of the army throughout the entire period of the American Revolution. He led it through good times and bad, against better trained, better equipped, and larger armies. He had to face the problems of desertion and defeat. At times his army seemed to disappear as a morning fog.

After defeating Cornwallis he turned in his commission, retired to farming, but the country's chaotic political condition was so perilous that in May 1786 he declared, "Something must be done, or the fabric must fall, for it is certainly tottering." He thought that it was a real question, "whether the Revolution must be considered a blessing or a curse." He presided over the Constitutional Convention that finally adopted our Constitution.

He was unanimously chosen president, but so indifferent were the original states to the national government that they had difficulty getting a quorum present in New York to declare him elected. Washington established a strong presidency, independent of Congress. At one time he refused to accede to Congress. He assumed the role of leader in foreign affairs, established tariffs for the regulation and protection of trade, assumed personal command of the army when it looked as if we might be involved in another war, established a national bank and currency, established a postal system, had the Federal Government assume the war debts of the individual states. He faced the same battles over the Constitution that the president presently is facing. Strict constructionists claimed that the government could not do anything unless authorized by the Constitution. When Washington and Hamilton wanted to start a national bank, Jefferson, a strict constructionist, said it was unconstitutional. Washington interpreted the Constitution differently and felt that they could do anything not prohibited by the Constitution.

We do not need to belabor the matter that Washington, for all of his problems, proved to be the one man who could organize and lead this country along the paths that Jefferson and Adams envisioned. While Adams may have been the founder of the American Revolution and Jefferson the best able to verbalize his faith, it was Washington who was able to put it all together in the establishment of this nation.

George Washington had personal qualities that enabled him to become great and to be known as the father of his country.

He answered the call of duty. George Washington would have made a good Boy Scout, for he lived out the pledge, "On my honor I will do my best to do my duty . . . to my country." When he was asked to head up the American forces against the British, he reluctantly accepted the call. After years of strenuous and arduous fighting he turned in his commission and retired to his Virginia plantation. Again he heard the call to serve his country at the Constitutional Convention. He answered a call yet another time to serve as president.

I must admit my own amazement over the fact that our government is considering doing away with the draft. Nobody wants to fight in a war or risk his life. But I cannot understand the idea of those who will receive the blessings of a nation like this, and then feel no sense of responsibility for answering its calls for service.

Before we are overly harsh on those who are unwilling to be drafted, let me ask how many of us answer calls of service in our own communities? Would each one of us participate in meetings to discuss the future of our cities? Is it that the calls are not big enough for us? Or do we feel it unimportant to fulfill civic responsibilities?

George Washington did not turn his country down. I really wonder if our country can survive with so many people priding themselves on being a part of that majority which does not speak or act. The silent majority damns itself by admitting its inactivity.

Washington served his country, not himself. Many try to combine service of self and service of country. In answering the call as leader of the military forces of the United States, Washington made it plain that he would not accept any salary, only his expenses. In his first inaugural address delivered in New York City he again made clear the fact that he would not accept a salary. This was in spite of the fact that he had to borrow money to get to New York for his inauguration.

Many like Washington put service above themselves. Harry Truman and Dwight Eisenhower entered the office as president of the United States with modest funds. In no way would they use the office or their position to increase their holdings. School teachers in the past have accepted low income from their city or their country, because they wanted to serve children. Many ministers have served with substandard wages because of their commitment to their task.

It seems as if this day is almost over. The teachers, ministers, and other public servants have seen too many football players, for whom a college had to devise a special nonacademic curriculum, making salaries of five and six figures and have seen women little better than prostitutes calling themselves actresses, all living in abundance and luxury.

In contrast, politicians, teachers, and preachers have grown tired of not being able to send their children to good colleges because their services do not bring in adequate salaries.

Washington's idealism gave rise to the dollar-a-year politician, to ceilings on profits during wars, and to those thousands who have served humanity through the Peace Corps. We are not going to have many more of this kind of people unless we see a change in the attitude of the public toward them.

Washington lived for principle—not party. The great bulk of his address is given to calling upon us to be Americans, not southerners, northerners, easterners, or westerners. He saw the danger that could come from limited loyalties and from party spirit. He warned politicians against serving their own districts rather than the nation as a whole.

As he brought his years of public service to an end, he was able to say, "In reviewing the incidents of my Administration, I am unconscious of intentional error."

Some of us have been distressed in recent years over party politics and lack of principles in our political arrangements.

The matter of school busing has struck me as rather ludicrous. I am hearing a great deal of talk about the matter of principles in busing children, that children should go to the schools nearest to them, and that there should be local control.

I cannot understand the argument against busing, for we in the South have been busing for generations. We bused Negro children all the way across the county so that we could maintain segregation. We bused children from good school districts to bad ones, because we wanted to maintain segregation. Now when the tables are turned on us and they are talking about busing to enforce integration, we are screaming about a matter of principle.

Many of us are standing on the sides and wondering when America is going to ever wake up and start fighting for principle instead of personal privilege and party politics.

Washington also gave evidence of a great religious faith. It is not the purpose of this chapter to document Washington's religious convictions. This can be done. Those who know much about the man know that he did not kneel to pray and that he did not normally take communion. We do know that he was a vestryman in the Episcopal church, and that his life was supported by the religious convictions that are reflected in his speeches. For our purpose here I would call to your attention one of his greatest statements made during his farewell address: "Let us with caution indulge the supposition that morality can be maintained without religion. Whatever may be conceded to the influence of refined education on minds of peculiar structure—reason and experience both forbid us to expect, that national morality can prevail in exclusion of religious principles." [9]

It was Washington who on his own initiative added the phrase, "So help me God," to the oath of office. It was on his own that he leaned over and kissed the Bible after the oath of office had been administered.

This does not mean to imply that Washington was a sectarian. As president, he was president of the whole country. In 1796, in drawing a treaty involving Mediterranean trade with Tripoli, a Moslem state, Washington stipulated the correct constitutional point that "The government of the United States of America is not, in any sense, founded upon the Christian religion." [10]

In speaking to the Catholics, he said, "I hope ever to see America foremost among nations in example of justice and liberality." To the Quakers in Philadelphia, "The liberty of conscience enjoyed by these states . . . is not only among the choicest of their blessings but also of their rights." To the Jewish congregation in Newport, "May the children of the stock of Abraham . . . enjoy the good will of the other inhabitants . . . for happily the government of the United States gives to bigotry no sanction, to persecution no assistance." [11]

Yesterday I heard a man on the radio talking about the fall of America. People are no longer saying that there may be a decline in the United States. Many have the attitude that this is already happening.

No possibility of reviving John Adams, George Washington, or Thomas Jefferson exists today. These men served their day and should be left in their graves. But God has put you and me here now. The Holy Spirit can guide us that we can be for our day what they were for theirs. We must pray, "God, give us men."

# John Adams

# Father of the Revolution

*This is a sermon that I prepared and preached immediately prior to my son Tom's leaving for overseas duty in the United States Army. He had recently graduated from law school and had in mind a career that would combine law and public service.*

*Because of these circumstances I preached the sermon as a personal letter to this outstanding young man, who has such high visions and great hopes.* TAF

Dear Tom:

I am so proud of you that you have graduated from college, finished law school, passed the bar exam. I know that it is your dream to use your education for the enrichment of mankind, and it is in your thoughts that perhaps you will go into politics.

You know that this will please me, for I see certain gifts in you which would seem to fit admirably for that type of vocation.

With this in mind I thought I would write you a rather lengthy letter about a political statesman whom I admire a great deal.

I am thinking of John Adams, the second president of the United States. Like you, Adams lived in revolutionary times. The British called him the "Father of the American Revolution." When you consider how the revolutionary leaders in our own time are loved and hated, it is easy to understand how the pioneers of the American Revolution would have had the same response, particularly when you realize that one-third of the people were pro-British, one-third pro-American, and the other one-third were on the fence.

27

Adams also experienced the French Revolution and saw its idealism and its great failure.

Like you, Adams was a man of deep religious conviction. History books say that he was a Unitarian. You know that I have respect for Unitarians and would in no way attack them. But it ought to be understood that Unitarians in Adams's day and Unitarians today are two different things.

Perhaps the best illustration of what has happened to words is in the fact that Thomas Jefferson, the third president of the United States, was called a Republican but is now considered to be the founder of the Democratic party. Republicans are now the conservatives. In those days they were the liberal party. Just as Republican has shifted its meaning, so the word Unitarian has shifted meaning. You might be interested in hearing Adams's own evaluation of the Christian faith. "The Christian religion is, above all the religions that ever prevailed or existed in ancient or modern times, the religion of virtue, equity, and humanity. Let the blackguard Paine say what he will; it is resignation to God, it is goodness itself to man." [1]

In writing to his friend, Benjamin Rush, a Philadelphia physician and patriot, Adams said, "The Christian religion, as I understand it, is the brightness of the glory and the express portrait of the eternal, self-existent, independent, benevolent, all-powerful and all-merciful Creator, Preserver and Father of the Universe. . . . It will last as long as the world. Neither savage nor civilized man could ever have discovered or invented it. Ask me now then whether I am a Catholic or Protestant, Calvinist or Armenian. As far as they are Christians, I wish to be a fellow disciple of them all." [2]

Perhaps you are interested in a little history. Adams was born in Braintree, Massachusetts, the son of a farmer. The name of the community was later changed to Quincy, because the community leaders seemed to feel that the Quincy family was a more representative family than the Adams. Yet the Adams family produced two presidents.

Young Adams attended Harvard, but you should not let that intimidate you. When he was there, there were only thirty students with six faculty members. It was thought that he might enter the Congregational ministry, but he thought that the dogmas of extreme Calvinism were too restrictive.

It would be helpful for every young man in this generation to catch some of the vision of the Adams scholarship. He remained a student all of his life. On one occasion he said, "I am resolved to rise with the sun and to study the Scriptures on Thursday, Friday, Saturday, and Sunday mornings, and to study some Latin author the other three mornings. Noons and nights I intend to read English authors."

Tom, your generation has a hang-up about what you think was the hang-up of the Puritans. Many moderns discount anything that Puritans say, because they think that they were totally antipleasure, antilove, antisex. This is a false notion. It is just like saying that all modern preachers are segregationists. There are a few segregationists, but not many. So there were some Puritans opposed to the pleasures of life.

Irving Stone understood Puritans. In his book *Those Who Love* he has Abigail Adams's father, a Puritan minister, say to Abigail, "It simply is not true that the Puritan disapproves of physical love, or passion between a man and woman. Neither is there truth in the thunderings from the pulpit that sexual love, except for the purposes of procreation, is sinful. That it is evil, or ugly, the work of the devil for which the participants will be fearfully punished by their conscience or their community. My dearest daughter, carnal knowledge between people who love each other is one of God's noblest works. The devil, if such there be, can debase love, if a woman gives her body for pay, or a man is aroused by intoxication or religious excess, such as we had in the Great Awakening. We Puritans are a hearty breed, though there are some who would destroy the joyous fulfillment of life. Of course, I don't need to add that fulfillment must come at the proper season. After marriage you must never let your passion for each other die." [3]

My son, your idealism reminds me so much of Adams's. From the very outset of his law practice he put principle above popularity. One of the most amazing evidences of this is related to the "Boston Massacre." During a riot in Boston in 1770 a group of British soldiers fired into a crowd of Americans. Five Americans were killed. John Adams was already known as a revolutionary. He was one who created riots. To the amazement of all except his closest friends he volunteered to defend Captain Prescott, the British officer involved. He won his case and secured an

acquittal. He fully expected the entire community to turn against
him for his stand. In his remarks to the jury he said, "Facts are
stubborn things. And whatever may be our wishes, our inclina-
tions, or the dictates of our passion, they cannot alter the state
of facts and evidence." [4] You are going to find it hard to make
decisions like this one. Do you defend an unpopular person representing an unpopular cause? Do you ask what it will do to your
reputation? Will it be your determination as a young lawyer to
defend those whose legal cause is right irrespective of what it
will do to your own popularity?

The same belief in principle that made Adams defend Captain
Prescott also made him a fierce fighter for independence. I wish
I had been able to take you to see the play *1776*. It portrays the
Continental Congress and the part that John Adams and Thomas
Jefferson played in it. The members of the Continental Congress
did not like John Adams. He kept pushing them for independence, and they were content just to meet. One of the songs in
the play says, "Sit down, John. Sit down, John. For God's sake,
John, sit down." John Adams felt that the worst thing that God
had done for him was to inflict him with the Continental Congress. He said that America could have withstood a plague or
an earthquake much more satisfactorily than the "diddle daddle"
Continental Congress.

One of the most significant features of this man's life was his
ability to recognize his strengths and limitations. This comes hard
to us all. When the Continental Congress finally agreed to have
a Declaration of Independence written, John Adams was put on
the committee to write it. Having been the great spokesman for
Independence, he was asked by the committee of five to write
the first draft of the Declaration. He knew that if he did the
Continental Congress would pick it to pieces because it hated
him so much. He also recognized that the Declaration would
have a greater chance of passing if written by a Virginian. Then
in a rare insight he said to Thomas Jefferson, "Besides you can
write ten times better than I can." So he prevailed upon Thomas
Jefferson to draw up the initial draft.

Adams's political beliefs were founded on a premise that taxa-
tion without representation could not be. He felt that the British
had no right to levy taxes on the colonies unless the colonies were
represented in Parliament.

Tom, you have feelings, and I agree with you, that the United States government has no right to tax the Negroes in the South or anywhere else unless they can vote. Therefore, we fought for voting rights. I, like you, feel very much the same way about the young people. I do not feel that the government has a right to ask them to offer their lives in military service and then tell them they are too immature to vote. If they are old enough to die for their country, having been drafted, they are old enough to have a voice in deciding whether we go to war or not.

Adams and Jefferson would have disagreed on one vital point. Jefferson, and I think your generation, son, had a very optimistic view of mankind. Jefferson felt that if you give people an education, kept them informed, they would vote the right way. Adams had no such illusion. He had seen the French Revolution and came to the conclusion, "Men are never good but through necessity." [5] He also said, "I am more and more convinced that Man is a dangerous creature, and that power whether vested in many or a few is ever grasping, and like the grave cries give, give." [6]

Adams believed in democracy, not because he believed that the general populace would be right, but because he felt that the political leadership was as apt to be wrong as the general populace, and that this political leadership needed a restraining hand.

Having seen mobs and even congregations and boards of officers swayed by emotional appeal and controlled by prejudice, I must agree with Adams. I do not believe that the common man or the political leader will do what is right just because he knows what is right. The only hope is to see that there is enough pressure from a large enough group to try to keep political leadership in line.

Tom, you are fortunate, as was John Adams, in your choice of a wife. Both of you married great women. Irving Stone's *Those Who Love* tells the story of the love and support Abigail gave to John.

Like Leslie, Abigail had a marvelous sense of humor. Her father, a Congregational minister, gave to each of his daughters the privilege of choosing the text for his sermon the Sunday following her marriage. Abigail's sister, Mary, chose Luke 10:42, that says, "Mary has chosen the good portion. . . ." When the time came for Abigail to choose the text on the Sunday after her marriage, she chose Matthew 11:18, "For John came neither eating nor drinking, and they say, 'He has a demon.'"

You might learn something from John's career as a diplomat. He and his son, John Quincy, probably contributed as much to American foreign diplomacy as any two men. He secured loans from foreign countries to support us, but he was also very tactless. Can you imagine the tension when he had to appear before King George to present his credentials to Great Britain? King George III tried to lessen the electricity in the room by making some mention of the fact that he knew John had lacked confidence in the French government. In reply Adams said, "I must avow to your Majesty that I have no attachment but to my own country." [7]

In addition to the problems created by his principles and his lack of tact, Adams, feeling that the Revolution may have been purposeless, faced discouragement. From the time of the American Revolution until 1788 there were riots, rebellions, a time of depression that would make the Great Depression of the thirties look like prosperity, lawlessness, weakness and inefficiency in government. Washington, Jefferson, Adams—all were in despair. In response to the tragedy of the post-Revolutionary period the Constitution was adopted and Adams became vice president under Washington. As the first vice president, he was also the first to criticize the job. He said of it, "My country has in its wisdom contrived for me the most insignificant office that ever the invention of man contrived or his imagination conceived. In addition the pay was niggardly, my salary a curiosity." [8]

In spite of having served as a member of the Continental Congress, ambassador, vice president, Adams was never a political being. He and his son were the only two presidents in our country's early history who were not re-elected for second terms. If you are interested, I will write you more about his son, John Quincy, at a later time.

Adams's trouble as president developed because of a split in his own party. Alexander Hamilton was party leader, and Hamilton favored going to war with the French. Tremendous popular sentiment supported Hamilton. He even went so far as to raise an army to do battle with the French. One hundred and twenty years after Adams, Woodrow Wilson faced the same problem. The American people wanted war with Germany. Wilson withstood the pressure. But Wilson and Adams were both called cowards and lost a great deal of political support because of their efforts at peacemaking. Adams realized he was committing political suicide, and so he said he wanted this inscription on his gravestone, "Here lies John Adams, who took upon himself the responsibility of peace with France in 1800." [9] Adams had running against him the most popular figure in America—Thomas Jefferson.

Adams sealed his own fate by signing a bill passed in Congress by his own party called the Alien and Sedition Act. Under the terms of this law an individual could be fined two thousand dollars and be sentenced to two years in prison if he "should write, print, utter, or publish . . . any false, scandalous and malicious writing or writings against the government of the United States, the members of Congress or the president." [10] As a result of this act one hundred people were arrested. James T. Callender of the Richmond *Examiner* was sentenced to nine months in prison. One editor was tried and convicted because he said "the President ought to be sent to a mad house." Another author was put in jail and was elected to Congress while he was in prison.

Spiro Agnew should learn from Adams's experience that trying to muzzle the press may seem popular, but it can backfire. The government and the press are both here to stay. Each has a function with regard to the other. Any attempt on the part of one to usurp the power of the other must be avoided.

Some consider freedom of the press to be a luxury. In law and in politics you will have to learn to live with the press no matter how fiercely it may attack you. You will have to accept the fact that a country without a free press has lost one of its most essential freedoms. But for the press to be free it must have the right to attack you with the same venom and prejudice that it may attack your enemy. You see, son, the problems of our day are similar to the problems that have been faced by great men before us.

You have been blessed with a son. Your present vocation in the army and your future vocations may take you away from your family, as Adams had to be away from his family. You will never lose your concern or your love. In one of his letters to Abigail, John wrote her about their children, "John Quincy has genius. And so has Charles. Take care that they don't go astray.

Fix their attention on great and glorious objects. Root out every little thing. Weed out every meanness. Make them great and manly. Teach them to scorn injustice, ingratitude, cowardice and falsehood. Let them revere nothing but religion, morality and liberty." [11]

You will lose many battles in your legal and political life. On various occasions you will lose them even though you were right. Small-minded people around you can defeat you. There are three classes of leaders. Some, like Adams, are guided by great and noble principles. Some have their principles dictated by popular opinion. Still others follow their passions. It is the second group that usually end up on top of political power. And those of you who are in the first group, the men of eternal principles, frequently find themselves opposed and defeated.

Adams's most serious defeat was not in his second battle for the presidency. In fact he did not campaign. He felt that the job should seek the man, not the man the job. His great defeat was related to the Declaration of Independence. He and Jefferson both felt that the Declaration should contain a statement that slavery would not be allowed in the newly formed country. Rutledge of South Carolina led the opposition. Rutledge pointed out that it was Boston ships, owned by Boston capitalists who brought the slaves from Africa to the colonies. A coalition of those who wanted to protect the shipping industry and those who wanted to protect their investment in slaves brought about the defeat of Adams and Jefferson on this issue. Short-sighted men were interested in present gain. Had Adams and Jefferson won their battle, there would have been no Civil War.

What I have learned in my life is that on issues like this, you have to be beaten time after time before there can be an ultimate victory. There will be many times in your life when you will cry to God, saying, "Why did you let me get beat?" Surely God knows that you are right in much that you stand for, but selfish, greedy, ambitious men will do to you what they did to Jefferson and Adams, even though it means the ultimate destruction of their own country.

In keeping with this, son, Adams never forgot the fact that existence is not just a temporal matter but is eternal. After the death of Abigail, Adams wrote Thomas Jefferson these words: "I do not know how to prove physically, that we shall meet and know each other in a future state, nor does Revelation, as I can find, give us any positive assurance of such a felicity. My reasons for believing it, as I do most undoubtedly, are that I cannot conceive such a being could make such a species as the human, merely to live and die on this earth. If I did not believe in a future state, I should believe in no God. This Universe, this all would appear, with all of its swelling pomp, a boyish firework. And if there be a future state, why should the Almighty dissolve forever all the tender ties which unite us so delightfully in this world, and forbid us to see each other in the next?" [12]

There have been times in your life when you have not thought much of the church and organized religion. You know that I have agreed with you. There have been several occasions when I have considered leaving the ministry. Maybe one of the reasons I like Adams so much is that he expressed so adequately my own feelings about the church and the faith. In another letter to Thomas Jefferson, he said, "Twenty times in the course of my late readings, have I been on the point of breaking out. 'This would be the best of all worlds if there were no religion in it!' But in this exclamation I should have been as fanatical as Bryant or Cleverly. Without religion, this world would be something not fit to be mentioned in polite company—I mean hell." [13]

As I have written you all of these things, my mind is turned back to a Biblical figure—Job. The book about him opens with these words, "One who feared God, and turned away from evil." If this could be said of Job, then surely it could be said even more of John Adams. In expressing his commitment to his own country and his faith, Adams once said, "All that I have, all that I am, all that I hope for in this life, I stake on our cause. For me the die is cast. Sink or swim, live or die, to survive or perish with my country is my unalterable resolution." [14]

You have chosen a noble course. I am very proud of you. No matter what you do, I will always love you and be thankful that you are my son.

In setting your goals, I should like so much for you to consider for one of your heroes John Adams, who fathered a revolution that gave birth to the greatest nation in the world. As you live through revolutionary times, I could have no nobler dream for you than that you be part of a creative revolution that would establish politically the fact that all men are created equal and are endowed by their Creator with inalienable rights and that among these are life, liberty, and the pursuit of happiness, and that governments are instituted to insure those rights.

I love you.

Your father.

# Thomas Jefferson

# Genius of Monticello

Margaret Bayard Smith had expected Thomas Jefferson to be violent, vulgar, bold, profligate. After she met him, she wrote, "Oh, he is a good man! And the day will come when all party spirit shall expire, that every citizen of the United States will join in saying, 'He is a good man.'" [1] Her words were an echo of those biblical words about Barnabas, "He was a good man."

This man, the third president of the United States, wrote his own epitaph. It says: "Here was buried Thomas Jefferson, author of the Declaration of Independence, of the Statute of Virginia for Religious Freedom, and Father of the University of Virginia." *Encyclopaedia Britannica* has given a more general and perhaps better description when it says, "He is the most conspicuous of American apostles of democracy."

Thomas Jefferson has been called, along with Leonardo da Vinci, "The universal man." Jefferson was an architect, engineer, public health campaigner, linguist, author, educator, paleontologist.

We can understand the sources of his knowledge when we read his advice to James Madison and James Monroe, two youthful neighbors and protégés who succeeded him as presidents of the United States. When they were students at William and Mary, he wrote them of his own schedule as a student. "From daybreak til eight in the morning, study the natural sciences. From eight to twelve, read law. From twelve to one, read politics. In the afternoon read history and the Bible. From dark to bedtime, literature, criticism, classic oratory." [2]

In contrast with Washington, Jefferson was a very successful family man. His marriage was a good one, even though it lasted only ten years. At his wife's grave he had inscribed these words from the *Iliad*: "If in the house of Hades men forget their dead, Yet will I even there remember you, dear companion." [3]

Just before she died Martha requested Jefferson not to marry again. Most historians feel that this was because she had been reared by a stepmother and did not want her children to suffer the indignities that she had experienced. Jefferson honored this request.

His relationship with his daughter is indicated by words written to him by the daughter, Martha, when she said that all the concerns in her life were secondary to her love for her husband, "except my love for you."

Richard Henry Lee and others of his friends chided Jefferson for his attachment to his family. The play *1776* communicates his love for his wife, but it is unfair in suggesting that he postponed writing the Declaration of Independence just to spend the day with her.

Jefferson was an expert violinist, good singer and dancer, proficient outdoor sportsman, excellent horseman, owner of thoroughbred horses. It is interesting to note that with these interests he never used tobacco, played cards, gambled, or became party to a personal quarrel.

One sidelight that makes me grateful to him is the fact that he introduced ice cream to America. It was a French delicacy that he brought back with him after his term as ambassador in France.

It is difficult to understand certain aspects of Jefferson's life until you are aware of the fact that he had terrible migraine headaches. At times these caused him to pull back and isolate himself from people.

I should also mention that he, like George Washington, had financial troubles. In 1826 Jefferson owed over one hundred thousand dollars. In order to pay off his debts he decided to sell his beloved Monticello in a national lottery. Instead, a national campaign was put on by some of his friends to help him with his debts. This raised something over sixteen thousand dollars, saving him from bankruptcy. Shortly after his death, his pictures, his furniture, his silver, and even Monticello were sold at auction to pay off his obligations.

Jefferson made great sums of money early in his life as a lawyer and as a farmer. He realized that he had to devote his life to something more important than making money. His salary and total expense account as president was twenty-five thousand dollars a year. The household expenses of running the White House, with all of its entertaining, cost him more than that. When he pledged his fortune to the establishment of this country, he meant it. I am not suggesting that he died in depression over his finances. I am sure that as he sat on the lawn of Monticello, there must have been some concern over his financial condition. I am also sure that as he looked down the mountain to the University of Virginia—as he looked out over the countryside thinking of the Constitution, Declaration of Independence, the Bill of Rights, the Virginia Statute for Religious Freedom—all of these things gave him more satisfaction than a million dollars could have. His treasure and his heart were in terms of personal values.

In what is reputed to have been one of the dirtiest presidential campaigns in American history, Thomas Jefferson was accused of being an atheist, of being immoral and anti-religious. After Jefferson's death the Rev. Mr. Bird Wilson said, "I believe the influence of his example and name has done more for the extension of infidelity than that of any other man."

Two primary forces are behind the accusations that he was an atheist. His theology was very little different from that of George Washington or the Adamses (father and son). It was not his theology but his acts that brought the wrath of the church upon him.

First of all he was responsible for the Virginia Statute of Religious Freedom. He felt that this was one of the three contributions of his own life. In essence it dis-established the Episcopal church, affirming the fundamental principle of separation of church and state for Virginia. This became part of the Bill of Rights of the United States. Clergymen whose state support and political influence were thereby cut did not like it one bit.

Another root of his problem with the church was his refusal to proclaim a national Thanksgiving day. George Washington had proclaimed such a day. During the lifetime of many of us Congress has made Thanksgiving an official national holiday and

has even set the specific time. Thomas Jefferson felt that this was
unconstitutional. To him it was the state supporting an ecclesiastical or religious observance.

Today we like to affirm the separation of church and state, but
I am not sure that we would be much happier with Thomas
Jefferson than many churchmen were in his own time.

We like the tax cover that Madalyn Murray O'Hair is attack-
ing. The Roman Catholic and the Baptist churches have large
property holdings. The Presbyterian church and the Methodist
church have less holdings because they are smaller. We seem to
be frightened over the fact that the state may not continue giving
us privileged tax positions.

Some of our people talk much about separation of church and
state but want the state to enforce sabbath laws. We fully expect
the Federal government to supply chaplains for the armed forces.
Laws of sabbath observance and armed forces chaplains both
seem to be violations of the principle of separation of church
and state and are probably in violation of the Constitution.

Can you imagine what would happen if the present president
of the United States came out favoring a removal of the tax cover
that protects the church and said that the proclamation of a
Thanksgiving day and laws concerning the sabbath and the
chaplaincy were unconstitutional, and that, therefore, he would
not support them?

I am sure that even President Nixon would be called an atheist
if he took the stands comparable to those taken by Thomas
Jefferson. Jefferson did not take these attacks without retaliation.
He once wrote, "My opinion is that there would never have been
an infidel, if there had never been a priest." [4]

In order to answer the question of whether or not Jefferson
was church oriented, one has to look at certain things he said
and did.

First of all he was a regular attendant at church. One author
points out that while Jefferson was president it was his consistent
habit to attend worship every Sunday. During the early period
of his presidency there were only two churches in Washington,
D.C.—a Roman Catholic church and a very small Episcopal
church. The Episcopal church was an old tobacco house that
had had slight modifications. The congregation had only fifty or

sixty members, and on many a Sunday only twelve to fourteen
attended the worship hour. Seldom were there over twenty. This
congregation was not made up of the elite, and there was no
political reason for his attending. He attended worship because
he believed in attending worship.

Nearly every president has had a hobby to divert himself from
the weight of the office. Eisenhower played golf. Truman went
fishing. Franklin D. Roosevelt kept a stamp collection. Thomas
Jefferson's diversion was Bible study. During his years in the
White House he compiled a harmony of the gospels, putting together the gospel message in a single narrative form. The earliest
title page of this volume read: "The philosophy of Jesus of Naza-
reth extracted from the account of his life and teaching as given
by Matthew, Mark, Luke and John being an abridgement of the
New Testament for the use of the Indians, unembarrassed with
matters of fact or faith beyond their comprehension." [5]

Later in his life, he said of his own faith, "I am a Christian in
the only sense in which He (Jesus) wished anyone to be." [6]

On another occasion he wrote, "The doctrines of Jesus are
simple and tend all to the happiness of man: 1. That there is only
one God and He all perfect. 2. That there is a future state of
rewards and punishments. 3. That to love God with all thy heart
and thy neighbor as thyself is the sum of religion." [7]

In his reaction against certain dogmas of the church, particularly the trinity and the miracles, one has to remember the
atmosphere of his time. He was reacting against the excesses of
the Great Awakening. God had been pictured as being a fierce
and vengeful God. Jesus was portrayed as being a sort of second
God who was opposed to the vengeance of God.

It was Jefferson's contention that a man's religious faith was
reflected in his life in the world. If this be so, then this man
was a man of great Christian faith.

A theologian would say that Jefferson believed man was made
in the image of God. I have run into no statement where Jefferson
used such language, but the very foundation of Jefferson's political philosophy was the worth of the individual. Need I remind
you of those magnificent words of the Declaration of Independence: "We hold these Truths to be self-evident, that all Men
are created equal, that they are endowed by their Creator with

certain inalienable Rights, that among these are Life, Liberty
and the Pursuit of Happiness—That to secure these Rights, Governments are instituted among Men, deriving their just Powers
from the Consent of the Governed. . . ." God created men and
gave them their rights. This faith gave birth to the battle against
the British. It also made him oppose slavery.

He carried his concept of the worth of man farther in seeking
to establish in Virginia a series of schools that would guarantee
every white male the opportunity of education. The capstone of
the educational system was to be the University of Virginia.

His critics thought the University of Virginia to be an atheistic
institution. It was common practice in universities in the nineteenth century to have departments of religion and Bible. He felt
that to establish such a department at the University of Virginia
with its expenses paid by the state would be a violation of the
constitutional provisions of the separation of church and state.
He was most anxious for the young men to have religious training, and so he provided that ground would be made available
immediately adjacent to the university to any and all groups to
establish their own departments of religion and that students of
the university would be able to take courses in these schools.
They could choose the course and the religious training that
suited them. This was the first manifestation of what has now
come to be known as the release time concept.

Jefferson's concept of man is reflected not only in the Declaration of Independence, but in his inaugural address as president of the United States. He listed as the first responsibility of
government: "equal and exact justice to all men, of whatever
state or persuasion, religious or political; peace, commerce, and
honest friendship with all nations . . ."

This emphasis upon the worth of the individual carried over
into the matter of freedom of press as well as freedom of religion.

We mentioned that John Adams and George Washington had
trouble with the press. Thomas Jefferson also had trouble. Spiro
Agnew has never had it so bad. They accused Jefferson of mis-
management, duplicity, immorality—even fathering children out
of wedlock. A German visitor, Baron Alexander von Humboldt,
found a newspaper in the waiting room at the White House that
carried many of these slanders. He picked it up and took it
with him when he went in to see Jefferson and asked, "Why is

not this libelous journal suppressed, or its editor at least fined and imprisoned?" Jefferson smiled. "Put that paper in your pocket, Baron, and should you hear the reality of our liberty, the freedom of the press, questioned, show this paper and tell where you found it." [8]

Jefferson also believed in the absoluteness of right and wrong, that justice is a reality, that sin would be punished. I have no quotation from Jefferson that reflects the words "wages of sin is death." There is a magnificent statement regarding the race issue. "Indeed I tremble for my country when I reflect that God is just; that His justice cannot sleep forever." [9]

Jefferson seemingly was aware that injustice may prevail and that concepts of injustice may carry the day, but it was his firm conviction that every injustice would at one time or another bring its punishment.

Many people seem to feel that if you can get by with sin now, you have gotten by with it. The only applause that you look for is present applause. There is no concept of a God who says, "Well done, thou good and faithful servant," or "Depart from me, you worker of iniquity."

The third reflection of Jefferson's faith was in his love for people and his love for his countrymen. We have called him the genius of Monticello. No one can understand Jefferson without understanding his depth of love for this one particular spot of American soil. Immediately around him were the young men he influenced like Madison and Monroe. In the distance was the University of Virginia. Close at hand was his family.

I cannot imagine Thomas Jefferson leaving Monticello to live in Australia or Canada. His heart was in his home. He would not abandon his home, its people, its country, and its friendships. They were too meaningful to him. When things became oppressive under the British, he sought to overthrow them. He would not have understood those of our own day who leave home and country to go to Scandinavia, Canada, Australia.

Nor could Jefferson have gone along with those signs that say, "America—love it or leave it." These signs imply that if you don't like it here, get out. Jefferson sought to change things. He did not like ignorance, and so he sought to build schools. He did not like bigotry, and so he wrote the Virginia Statute of Religious Freedom.

Those who say, "America—love it or leave it," would have said to Thomas Jefferson, "Get out and go somewhere else." But Jefferson loved his country, and he loved it enough to give his life to changing it to be a country after his God's own will.

As I look back on Jefferson's life, I find certain inconsistencies. He was a strict Constructionist, feeling that the executive branch had no power except that which was specifically delineated in the Constitution. But when the opportunity came to buy Louisiana, he went against his constitutional principles and secured this western territory for us.

I point this out simply to emphasize that Jefferson really had two great loves and aims, and that throughout his life he had to blend these two. The first was a love for God and idealism. This is reflected in all of his official documents from the Declaration of Independence on down through statements from his retirement home at Monticello. But the second was his abiding love for his country. He vacillated as he sought to keep these two together.

On July 3, just before Jefferson died on July 4, he called his daughter, Martha, into the room and handed her a little box. In it was a poem that he had written:

> Life's visions are vanished, its dreams are no more
>   Dear friend of my bosom, why bathed in tears?
> I go to my Father's: I welcome the shore
>   Which crowns all my hopes or which buries my cares.
> Then farewell, my dear, my lov'd daughter, adieu!
>   The last pang of life is in parting from you!
> Two seraphs await me long shrouded in death;
>   I will bear them your love on my last parting breath.[10]

The two seraphs who would be waiting for him were his wife, Martha, and his daughter, Maria.

Jefferson had been invited to be a part of a Fourth of July program in honor of the fiftieth anniversary of the Declaration of Independence. Because of his ill health, he had to decline the invitation. On July 3 he slept. About seven o'clock in the evening, he woke up, and said, "This is the fourth of July." His descendants who were around him told him, "no." Again later, he asked, "This is the Fourth?" Finally after repeating the question several times, the hands of the clock showed it was July 4, 1826. When told it was the fourth he replied, "ah," and fell into sleep again. Fifty minutes later he was dead.[11]

A few hours after this John Adams, his close friend and fellow president, lay dying. Both of them died July 4, 1826. Adams had not heard of Jefferson's death and his last words were, "Thomas Jefferson still survives." [12]

We are not concerned about raising up new Thomas Jeffersons or George Washingtons, but we are deeply concerned that there be men of our day who will make as full a commitment of their lives to the God in whom they believe as Jefferson made to his God—a man about whom it could be said, " He [is] a good man."

God give us men! A time like this demands
  Strong minds, great hearts, true faith and ready hands;
Men whom the lust of office does not kill;
  Men whom the spoils of office cannot buy;
Men who possess opinions and a will;
  Men who have honor, men who will not lie;
Men who can stand before a demagogue
  And damn his treacherous flatteries without winking;
Tall men, sun crowned, who live above the fog
  In public duty and in private thinking.[13]
                        Josiah Holland

# John Quincy Adams

# The Servant of His God

JUST THIS WEEK I have organized the Loyal Order
of Job. It is named for the man in the Bible who lost his wealth,
health, and family but still maintained the integrity of his soul
and his relationship to his God.

An honorary member of that society should be John Quincy
Adams, the sixth president of the United States. Late in his
career, he wrote: "My whole life has been a succession of disappointments. I can scarcely recollect a single instance of success
to anything that I ever undertook." [1] In speaking of his future,
he said: "I have no plausible motive for wishing to live when
everything I foresee and believe of futurity makes death desirable, and when I have the clearest indications that it is near
at hand." [2]

This remarkable statement about the futility of his past life
was written by a man who had served his country as ambassador,
senator, secretary of state, and president, and who had been the
president's instrument in securing Florida from Spain and had
developed what is now known as the Monroe Doctrine. Historians
say that Adams's most significant days were after he had made
this statement indicating that his life seemed to be over.

Over the entrance of his burial spot was placed this inscription,
"Born a citizen of Massachusetts. Died a citizen of the United
States." [3]

John Quincy Adams lived "four lives." He was born in Braintree, Massachusetts on July 11, 1767. He was named after his
mother's grandfather, John Quincy. He traveled in Europe with
his father while his father was ambassador. At the age of fourteen

he became private secretary to Francis Dana, American envoy to Russia. He came back to this country, graduated from Harvard, then served as a foreign minister until his father was defeated for the presidency by Thomas Jefferson. He resigned, lest Thomas Jefferson feel it imperative to recall him. Thus at thirty-three, he ended the first phase of his life, already having accomplished more than most men do in their entire lives.

He became state senator and almost immediately United States senator. He was most unpopular as a senator. His party, the Federalist, strongly opposed the acquisition of Louisiana. He voted with the Republicans for this purchase. During the French and English War he backed President Jefferson's call for an Embargo Act. This hurt New England's shipping industry, and so his party strongly opposed it. He said in his diary: "A politician in this country must be the man of a party. I would fain be the man of my whole country." He said to another senator, "This measure will cost you and me our seats, but private interest must not be put in opposition to public good." [4]

The Federalist party in Massachusetts was so unhappy with him that they elected a senator to succeed him, even before his senate term was completed. Thus at forty years of age, he had completed the second phase of his life.

He started all over in the third phase of his life. He accepted a teaching position at Harvard. From this spot he moved to ambassador, secretary of state, and finally president of the United States. During these years he negotiated for the purchase of Florida from Spain, developed the Monroe Doctrine, established the Smithsonian Institution. During his presidency his own party did not support him because he refused to indulge in patronage. He would not fire a man because he was of the opposite party, nor would he employ a man because he was of his own party. This meant that his own party had little to gain from supporting him. Andrew Jackson was thus able to beat him when he tried for a second term as president. This defeat marked the end of the third period of John Quincy Adams's life.

It was then that he wrote the evaluation, "My whole life has been a succession of disappointments. I can scarcely recollect a single instance of success to anything that I ever undertook." And also the statement, "I have no plausible motive for wishing to live when everything I foresee and believe of futurity makes death desirable, and when I have the clearest indications that it is near at hand."

Shortly thereafter a group of his neighbors came to him and asked if he would consider allowing them to run him for the office of congressman from that district. Some suggested that it would be a degrading experience to serve in Congress after having been president. He said: "No person could be degraded by serving the people as a Representative in Congress. Nor, in my opinion, would an ex-President of the United States be degraded by serving as a selectman of his town, if elected thereto by the people." 5

He ran on the basis that he would not campaign in his own behalf. Of his election to Congress he said: "My election as President of the United States was not half so gratifying to my inmost soul. No election or appointment conferred upon me ever gave me so much pleasure." 6

Throughout Adams's life his sense of duty and responsibility dominated him. He once said: "I implore that Spirit from whom every good and perfect gift descends to enable me to render essential service to my country, and that I may never be governed in my public conduct by any consideration other than that of my duty." 7

This sense of responsibility was actually broader than to his country, for his father laid down the text of John Quincy's own life when he said, "The magistrate is the servant not . . . of the people but of his God." 8

Many of us are disturbed över moral decay that marks the day. Personally, I am not as distressed over breached moral codes as I am of the very atmosphere in which we are living. The chief goal of life seems to be pleasure. Let me be specific. I am distressed over a large segment of our ladies. Many who complete the rearing of their children feel that from then on out the whole purpose of life is to be a "clothes horse," to enjoy herself, to attend parties and lap up the goodies of the days. John Quincy Adams raised for himself the question that I think needs to be asked by every one of us, "What have I done with the seventy-four years that I have been indulged with the blessing of life?" This question needs to be asked by every retired man. Has he

retired so he can go fishing, play golf, or so that he can adequately fulfill the destiny for which God has created him?

Those of us who are working must ask the same question.
Is our work a worthy fulfillment of our nature and of the life
that God has given us, or are we just working so that we can
make money to clothe ourselves so that we can work?

From the earliest days of the Protestant Reformation our
emphasis was upon the parable of the talents. Out of the Reformation came capitalism and puritanism, both of which were
based upon the individual's accountability to God for the way
in which he had spent his life.

Some may suggest that John Quincy Adams was neurotic or
that he had a Messianic complex. But our world would be so
much better off today if more of us would worry about violating
the trust that God has given to us.

John Quincy Adams's sense of justice and equity made him
admired even by his enemies. I have seen a Bible that was presented to Adams by a group of black Africans. But perhaps I
had best tell you their story.

Many of the laws of the eighteenth century were such that
if a black African got off a boat and came ashore in an American
harbor, it was possible for him to be picked up, held, and sold
as a slave.

This particular group came into Boston. They were assured
that they could come ashore without danger. Too late they found
that they had been tricked.

John Adams defended these men in the American court to the
embarrassment of the ship owners, many slave holders, and
dealers in human flesh. As a token of appreciation they gave
him this Bible that I have seen. They inscribed in it, "The
Honorable John Quincy Adams. Most Respected Sir: The Mendi
people give you thanks for all your kindness to them. They will
never forget your defense of their rights before the Great Court
at Washington. They feel that they owe to you, in a large measure, their deliverance from the Spaniards, and from Slavery or
Death. They will pray for you, Mr. Adams, as long as they
live . . . May God bless and reward you! For The Mendi People,
Cinque, Kinna, Hale, Boston, November 6, 1841."

His tremendous sense of justice caused him to be the one-
man symbol of the struggle against slavery.

Many times I have agreed with Karl Marx that "religion is the opiate of the people." I do not like much of the devotional material that is used, for too often it is the sickly, soupy, ineffective religious "mumbo-jumbo" that is used to deaden the sensitivities and to emasculate the purposes and programs of the faith.

John Quincy Adams received a challenge from his faith that was as broad as mankind and is as inclusive as the words "God so loved the world."

He was concerned over the matter of public worship. On May 27, 1838, he wrote: "The neglect of public worship in this city [Washington] is an increasing evil, and the indifference to all religion throughout the whole country portends no good. There is in the clergy of all the Christian denominations a timeserving, cringing, subservient morality, as wide from the spirit of the Gospel as it is from the intrepid assertion and indication of truth. The counterfeit character of a very large portion of the Christian ministry of this country is disclosed in the dissensions growing up in all the Protestant churches on the subject of slavery. . . . This question of slavery is convulsing the Congregational Churches in Massachusetts: It is deeply agitating the Methodists; it has already completed a schism in the Presbyterian Church." [9]

The criticism here is of a ministry that had allowed the church to remain blind to the moral issues and had not guided the people. The same complaint could be made today. The churches are dividing now because for over one hundred years the ministry has remained silent when it should have spoken. If the church had been speaking God's word for the last one hundred years, then our people would not be so shocked when they heard the truth today.

John Quincy Adams loved the Bible. In his diary on September 26, 1810, he said:

"I have made it a practice for several years to read the Bible through in the course of every year. I usually devote to this reading the first hour after I rise every morning. As, including the Apocrypha, it contains about fourteen hundred chapters, and as I meet with occasional interruptions, when this reading is for single days, and sometimes for weeks, or even months, sus-

pended, my rule is to read five chapters each morning, which
leaves an allowance of about one-fourth of the time for such
interruptions. Extraordinary pressure of business seldom inter-
rupts more than one day's reading at a time. Sickness has frequently occasioned longer suspensions, and travelling still more
and longer. During the present year, having lost very few days,
I have finished the perusal earlier than usual. I closed the book
yesterday. As I do not wish to suspend the habit of allowing
regularly this time to this purpose, I have this morning com-
menced it anew, and for the sake of endeavoring to understand
the book better, as well as giving some variety to the study, I
have begun this time with Ostervald's French translation, which
has the advantage of a few short reflections upon each
chapter." [10]

It was said of him, "no man could read the Bible with such
powerful effect, even with the cracked and winded voice of old
age." [11]

Adams describes to us his characteristic daily regimen in the
White House, on December 31, 1825:

"I rise usually between five and six—that is, at this time of
the year, from an hour and a half to two hours before the sun.
I walk by the light of moon or stars, or none, about four miles,
usually returning home in time to see the sun rise from the
eastern chamber of the House. I then make my fire, and read
three chapters of the Bible, with Scott's and Hewlett's Commen-
taries. Read papers till nine. Breakfast, and from ten till five
P.M. receive a succession of visitors, sometimes without inter-
mission, very seldom with an interval of half an hour—never
such as to enable me to undertake any business requiring attention. From five to half-past six we dine; after which I pass about
four hours in my chamber alone, writing in this diary, or reading
papers upon some public business—excepting when occasionally
interrupted by a visitor. Between eleven and twelve I retire to
bed, to rise again at five or six the next morning." [12]

Today America honors one that the newspapers branded as
"the mad man from Massachusetts," a man who was removed
from the Senate by his own state, failed to be re-elected as

President, who was almost censured by Congress. The *Salem Gazette* said "that he was a popularity seeker." The *New Hampshire Gazette* once said of him, "He was a party scavenger!" [13] A leading Boston citizen said he would not sit at the same table with that renegade.

I would not suggest to you that America needs another John Quincy Adams. We do need you, and need for you to make the same commitment and enter into life with the same sense of responsibility that marked the life of John Quincy Adams. The Holy Spirit does not guide any two of us into exactly the same position. There is something distinctive for each of us to do.

I am confident that if we will follow the Scriptural injunction to "let a man examine himself" we will ask what we have done to deserve the life and the goodness that has been bestowed upon us. I hope we will commit our life to God. Then we can be for our generation what John Quincy Adams was for his.

When toward the end of his life he entered the House of Representatives, every man arose to his feet. They called him "old man eloquent." He had a stroke in this same room two days before he died. Senator Thomas Hart Benton remarked, "Where could death have found him but at the post of duty?" [14]

# Abraham Lincoln

# A Man for All People

ABRAHAM LINCOLN may seem to be a strange subject for a sermon from a Christian pulpit, for he never officially joined a Christian church. Two things should be said about this.

First, any study of the church of the first half of the nineteenth century will indicate that it was at one of its lowest periods of spiritual strength. Early in his political life Abraham Lincoln took a stand against slavery. It was a shock to me to know that at the time of the outbreak of the War between the States 5,000 Methodist ministers owned 219,000 slaves (over 43 per minister); and 1,400 Episcopal priests owned 88,000 slaves (about 63 slaves for each priest). It is not Presbyterian pride that keeps me from giving the figures for our denomination. I was not able to locate information concerning the Presbyterians and their slaves. With the church so morally blind, is it any wonder that it had no appeal for a man who had such high ideals. Lincoln once said: "When any church will inscribe over its altar as its sole qualification for membership the Master's condensed statement of the substance of both the Law and the Gospel, 'Thou shalt love the Lord thy God with all thy heart, soul, mind and strength, and thy neighbor as thyself,' that church will I join with all my heart. . . ."

It should also be said that Abraham Lincoln, while not being a member of the church, was one of our most deeply devout presidents. In the Washington Cathedral in the nation's capital, one of the great monuments to him stands. It is entitled "Lincoln at Prayer." It was executed by Herbert Houck, whose grandfather once discovered Lincoln in one of the fields near Gettysburg, kneeling among the leaves. His use of the Scriptures, his vision of the Civil War in terms of punishment for sin, his

prayer and worship habits were public testimonials to the great
faith of this man. He had special qualities that single him out as
a spiritual giant.

Was not Lincoln one of history's greatest examples of the
words of our Lord when he opened the Sermon on the Mount
by saying, "Blessed are the meek, for they shall inherit the
earth"?

At a luncheon meeting recently Congressman Jim Wright told
of one of Lincoln's cabinet members who happened to come upon
a group of men discussing gorillas. The cabinet member said,
"The original gorilla is in the White House. If you want to see
him, go down there and look in, and you will see him sitting
there scratching himself."

General George McClelland treated Lincoln no better. When
McClelland was in charge of the army of the Potomac, Lincoln
went to see him to discuss a matter of strategy with him. McClelland was out. Lincoln waited. An hour later McClelland arrived,
saw Lincoln sitting there, and went upstairs. After thirty minutes
McClelland had not returned, and so President Lincoln sent a
servant to tell him he wanted to see him. The servant returned,
saying that he was sorry, but General McClelland was tired and
had gone to bed.

Such an attitude would have destroyed the relationship between any other president and his general, but when someone
asked Mr. Lincoln about McClelland, he said, "I will hold McClelland's horse, if he will only bring us success."

Here was a man of true humility. This humility is illustrated
in his second inaugural address where he said: "Both read the
same Bible, and pray to the same God; and each invokes his
aid against the other. It may seem strange that any men should
dare to ask a just God's assistance in wringing their bread from
the sweat of other men's faces but let us judge not that we be
not judged. The prayers of both could not be answered—that
of neither has been answered fully. . . . With firmness in the
fight, as God gives us to see the right, let us strive on to finish
the work we are in."

There is nothing in these words of the cocksure attitude that
the speaker holds all the truth. Just the opposite. He said, "Both
read the same Bible and pray to the same God. . . . Let us judge

not that we be not judged." He then added, "with firmness in the fight as God gives us to see the right." Can you imagine this coming from any recent president of the United States? We have the feeling that to be a strong leader you have to know that you are right and that the other man is absolutely wrong. We feel that we have to believe that all of God's truth is on our side. It is no wonder that many of Lincoln's own cabinet members and his general took advantage of him, made fun of him, snubbed him. But his cabinet is known no longer, while he has joined his place among the heroes of world history.

Lincoln is not only known for his humility, but for his graciousness toward his enemy. Those of us whose ancestors suffered during the horrible days of the carpetbaggers and the reconstruction are well aware of the fact that had not Lincoln been assassinated, the story in the South would have been vastly different. The peace terms that General Grant inflicted upon General Lee were but reflections of Lincoln's generosity and graciousness. Those peace terms had three simple statements:

1. The enlisted men were to surrender their arms.
2. The officers were allowed to retain their arms.
3. All the soldiers were to go home and promise not to fight the government again.

So touched was Lee with the generosity of the terms that he said, "This will have a very happy affect upon my army." When Lee told Grant that the horses the soldiers used were not the government's but their own, Grant gave them permission to keep their horses, so they could take them back home and start plowing their crops again.

Perhaps the noblest expression of his generosity was in his second inaugural address when he said: "With malice toward none, with charity for all . . . let's strive to finish the work we are in; to bind up the nation's wounds; to care for him who had fought the battle, for his widow and his orphan."

Herbert Hoover, who was to be president of the United States representing Lincoln's party, said many years later, "We can have peace, or we can have revenge, but we cannot have both."

While great preachers like Henry Ward Beecher called upon Lincoln to punish the South, it was Lincoln's desire to bind wounds. How reminiscent we are of those words of our Lord's own inaugural address: "He has sent me to proclaim release to the captives . . . to set at liberty those who are oppressed."

The South was prone to forget the proposal that Lincoln submitted to his cabinet when it appeared that the South was defeated. He wanted to request that Congress appropriate $400,000,000—an unimaginable sum for that day—which would be used to purchase at fair market value, every slave in the southern states. He said that freeing slaves was the equivalent of taking the property of the South, and the South was due recompense for it. He felt that this would give the South the influx of money that would be so necessary to get it on its feet again. The man's graciousness to a defeated enemy was not accepted by the cabinet. They voted unanimously against his recommendation. Did not Lincoln learn this from our Savior who said, "Love your enemies . . . pray for those who despitefully use you?"

The weight of the presidency was heavy upon his shoulders. When asked how it felt to be president of the United States, he said: "If being the head of Hell is half as hard as I have to undergo here, I would find it in my heart to pity Satan himself."

Lincoln never saw life as something given to be spent in seeking for one's own happiness. Life was a responsibility given by God. To use the words of our Lord, "We are to seek first the kingdom of God and His righteousness." To use the words of our catechism, "Man's chief end is to glorify God and enjoy Him forever."

No higher expression of this is found than in the Gettysburg address:

". . . we can not dedicate—we can not consecrate—we can not hallow—this ground. The brave men, living and dead, who struggled here, have consecrated it, far above our poor power to add or detract. The world will little note, nor long remember what we say here, but it can never forget what they did here. It is for us the living, rather, to be dedicated here to the unfinished work which they who fought here have thus far so nobly advanced. It is rather for us to be here dedicated to the great task remaining before us—that from these honored dead we take increased devotion to that cause for which they gave the last full measure of devotion—that we here highly resolve that these dead shall not have died in vain—that this nation, under God, shall have a new birth of freedom—and that government of the people, by the people, for the people, shall not perish from the earth."

Man's chief end is not to seek peace or pleasure but to fulfill the responsibility which God has given to him. Have we dedicated ourselves to seeing that the world for which they died has fulfilled their high vision, or have we been content to make our pile of money, to get our nice homes, to keep ourselves comfortable? Did the buddy who died next to you die so that you could live like you do now and so the world would be what it is now, or did he die in hopes that you and I would give ourselves to something better? Do you think that Christ died for you to be like you are now, or did he die to make you something better than you are? Lincoln did not look upon life as a means of self-gratification, but rather as a means of self-giving.

Lincoln's law partner, Herndon, pointed out that this sense of responsibility in Lincoln had many facets. Even though he was a very unattractive man physically, the women seemed to flock to him. He once said that a woman was the only thing he was afraid of that he knew could not hurt him. But it was Lincoln's sense of respect and honor that saved many a woman, or so says Herndon, where their own attitudes would have gladly given him permission to have and to destroy them morally and spiritually.

When he went into Richmond after the fall of the city, a group of Negroes gathered around him. It was a touching scene. Some of them felt that he was the Messiah. He spoke to them, saying: "My poor friends, you are free—free as air. You can cast off the name of slave and trample upon it; it will come to you no more. Liberty is your birthright. God gave it to you as he gave it to others, and it is a sin that you have been deprived of it for so many years. But you must try to deserve this priceless boon. Let the world see that you merit it, and are able to maintain it by your good works. Don't let your joy carry you into excesses. Learn the laws and obey them; obey God's commandments and thank him for giving you liberty, for to him you owe all things."

He saw liberty as a prize, also the beginning of responsibility for himself and those around him. Does not this remind you of our Lord's words, "To him to whom much is given, of him much will be required?"

Need I remind you that Lincoln was a man of peace? As a man from the deep South whose every known ancestor comes from the heart of Dixie, I am ashamed and humiliated that my forefathers would not tell the truth about Lincoln. The war-mongering papers in South Carolina and Alabama did not report honestly his first inaugural address. In that speech, he addressed the South and said: "In your hands, my dissatisfied fellow-countrymen, and not in mine, is the momentous issue of civil war. The government will not assail you. You can have no conflict without being yourselves the aggressors. You have no oath registered in heaven to destroy the government, while I shall have the most solemn one to 'preserve, protect, and defend it.' I am loath to close. We are not enemies, but friends. We must not be enemies. Though passion may have strained, it must not break our bonds of affection."

The whole effort of Lincoln's early administration was to bring peace. I know of no great public proclamation that he made during his administration that he would meet with southern leaders to bring peace. Word came to him that leaders of the South would like to meet and discuss peace. Without fanfare, he rushed to the Potomac, got into a boat, hurried to Hampton Roads, Virginia, to meet with three spokesmen of the Confederacy. *The New York Herald,* hearing about it, denounced Lincoln for his peace talk, but Lincoln's heart bled at the thought of two hundred or two thousand men dying every day. He once said, "I have never suffered by the South. I have suffered with the South. Their pain has been my pain. Their loss has been my loss."

Francis of Assisi put it most beautifully when he said, "Lord, make me an instrument of thy peace."

One greater than Francis said, "Blessed are the peacemakers for they shall be called the children of God." I wish that he had said, "Blessed are those who believe in the Scriptures, for they shall be called children of God," or, "Blessed are those who accept the Virgin Birth, for they shall be called the children of God." But he said, "Blessed are the peacemakers." Are you an instrument of peace? Is your neighbor an instrument of peace?

Is your church an instrument of peace? Is your world an instrument of peace?

One day a little girl stumbled and fell. Lincoln picked her up and was seeking to comfort her. He asked her what her name was, and she told him, "Mary Tuft." "Well, Mary, when you reach home, tell your mother you have rested in Abraham's bosom." Of course this tremendous respect for people was the thing behind Lincoln's position on slavery. In the earliest days of his political career, he introduced a bill into the Illinois Legislature to outlaw slavery. In a speech during the Great Debates he said, "A nation cannot exist half slave, and half free." In another place he said, "As I would not be a slave, so I would not be a master." On more than one occasion he compared slavery to "Snakes in a children's bed." He said, "If there was a bed newly made up to which the children were to be taken, and it was proposed to take a basket of young snakes to be put there with them, I take it no man would say there was any question how I ought to decide."

In considering the Emancipation Proclamation, Lincoln said, "Whatever shall appear to be God's will, I will do."

One of Lincoln's favorite expressions was, "In this country one man is as good as another and sometimes a little bit better." It was upon this concept of man made in the image of God, a creature to be respected and loved, that the great statement of the Declaration of Independence was born, "We hold these truths to be self-evident: That all men are created equal; that they are endowed by their Creator with certain inalienable rights; that among these are life, liberty, and the pursuit of happiness. . . ."

We might ask ourselves how we will be known. Will we be known as persons who have loved their fellow-man, or as good Samaritans, or as followers of him who said, "He has sent me to proclaim release to the captives . . . to set at liberty those who are oppressed"?

While Lincoln gave his life to freeing the slaves and risked everything he had for this, he put the issue of salvation of the union of the United States as the number one problem of his day. In August 1862 he wrote an open letter to Horace Greeley, editor of the *New York Tribune*: "My paramount object in this struggle is to save the Union, and is not either to save or to destroy slavery. If I could save the Union without freeing any slave, I would do it; and if I could save it by freeing all the slaves, I would do it; and if I could save it by freeing some and leaving others alone, I would also do that."

People have forgotten that Lincoln's primary concern was to save the Union. The preservation of the home, the city, or the state may be more important than the principles for which we are fighting. This is the thing that disturbs me about so much of the trouble in our city during the "long hot summer." If those who want opportunity and freedom create such situations of rioting and destruction as to destroy the very economy and government that has brought us to this hour, they will find a most hollow victory.

I am aware that there are problems in the ghettos and problems with our young people, but they are blind if they think that by destroying the government, the economy, and the social structure that has moved us thus far, they can attain their goals.

Without the Union, freedom would mean nothing. Lincoln knew that if he could maintain the Union, freedom might be slow in coming, but it would come.

Last summer when a riot seemed possible for Dallas I reminded you of one of Lincoln's early statements regarding law. Those words should be heard again: "Let reverence for the laws be breathed by every American mother to the lisping babe that prattles on her lap—let it be taught in schools, in seminaries, and in colleges; let it be written in primers, spelling books, and in Almanacs; let it be preached from the pulpit, proclaimed in legislative halls, and enforced in the courts of justice. And, in short, let it become the political religion of the nation; and let the old and young, rich and poor, the grave and gay, of all sexes, tongues, and colors and conditions, sacrifice unceasingly upon its altars."

On another occasion Lincoln said, "There is no grievance that is fit object of redress by mob law." At still another time in his career he said, "Among free men there can be no successful appeal from ballot to bullet."

We like to talk of law and obedience to law. But all too often it is with the idea of pointing our finger at the other man. We think nothing of walking across the street when the light says

stop, or of asserting our demands to travel to foreign countries
in spite of the President's appeal. The appeal of law must be
universal. Did not Jesus say, "I have not come to destroy the
law, but to fulfill?" The Scriptures tell us that the Christian
ought to be subject to the state. Lincoln set us a worthy example.

One of the most oft quoted statements about Lincoln is a
recounting of the number of times he seemed to fail. His record
is as follows:

> Lost job 1832.
> Defeated for legislature 1832.
> Failed in business 1833.
> Elected to legislature 1834.
> Sweetheart died 1835.
> Had nervous breakdown 1836.
> Defeated for Speaker 1838.
> Defeated for nomination for Congress 1843.
> Elected to Congress 1846.
> Lost renomination 1848.
> Rejected for land officer 1849.
> Defeated for Senate 1854.
> Defeated for nomination for Vice-President 1856.
> Again defeated for Senate 1858.
> Elected President 1860.

His abiding faith was well summed up in this comment which
he made after becoming President: "God selects His own instruments, and sometimes they are queer ones; for instance, He
chose me to steer the ship through a great crisis."

With Abraham Lincoln, you too can learn to say, "With God's
help I shall not fail." I do not know whether Lincoln even quoted
the verse, but I think we could apply certain words of Scripture
to him, "Be of good courage. I will not fail thee nor forsake thee."

As he left his friends in Springfield, he said to them, "Trusting
in Him who can go with me, and remain with you . . . let us
confidently hope."

I would never suggest that any of us try to emulate Abraham
Lincoln. I would call upon you to let Jesus Christ shine through
your life, as Lincoln let him shine through his life in his time.
The day of challenge and opportunity is not over.

Jesus Christ came into the world to save sinners. One sinner

who confessed his Lord with his mouth and with his deeds was
Abraham Lincoln. There is no doubt in my mind that Lincoln
subconsciously took for his platform the same words that my
Lord took when he said, "The spirit of the Lord is upon me
because he has anointed me to proclaim release for the captives
. . . to set free those who are oppressed."

That Lincoln's dream was not fulfilled was not his fault, but
the fault of the nation and the people who did not or would not
share his dream. That the dream of "one nation under God with
liberty and justice for all" has not become a reality, even in our
own day, is again not the fault of the leadership, but of the
people.

# Woodrow Wilson

# God's Man of the Hour

W<small>HEN THE WORLD NEEDS A MAN</small> to bring it to its senses, to redeem it from its sins, to point to the path of hope, God always raises up such a man.

The world seemed to come of age at the beginning of our century. The growth of industry, new scientific advances, the development of the medical profession, the blossoming of education, the increased wealth—all of these opened to man the glorious privilege of new days of prosperity, opportunity, justice, and peace.

God raised up Thomas Woodrow Wilson to lead us. He had the vision, the ability, the position; but the blindness and pettiness of his opposition kept our world from finding the way. Man's failure to follow the vision of Woodrow Wilson led to the Great Depression, the rise of an antagonistic Russia, World War II, and their aftermaths.

Had Wilson been followed in sincerity and in understanding, these chaotic and destructive events might have been avoided.

Wilson was right when he said, "Our civilization cannot survive materially unless it be redeemed spiritually." [1] His biographer, Josephus Daniels, quotes him as saying, "Christianity has liberated the world, not as a system of ethics, not as a philosophy of altruism, but by its revelation of the power of pure and unselfish love. Its vital principle is not its code, but its motive. Love, clearsighted, loyal, personal, is its breath and immortality. Christ came, not to save himself assuredly, but to save the world. His motive, His example is every man's key to his own gifts and happiness."

Woodrow Wilson was born in Staunton, Virginia, on Decem-

ber 28, 1856. His father was pastor of the Presbyterian church
there. When Wilson was two years old his father accepted a call
to be the pastor of the First Presbyterian Church in Augusta,
Georgia. Later he served as professor of what is now Columbia
Theological Seminary, pastor of the First Presbyterian Church,
Wilmington, North Carolina, and professor at Southwestern
which is now in Memphis, Tennessee. For thirty-three years he
was Stated Clerk of the General Assembly of the Presbyterian
Church, U.S.

Woodrow Wilson at seventeen entered Davidson College, became secretary of the Eumenean Literary Society. While a student at Davidson, he established a new record. When the chapel
bells started to ring, the tolling would wake him up. He was
able to dress, go all the way across the campus, and take his
seat in the chapel before the bell stopped ringing. No other man
in the history of Davidson has accomplished this feat. He tried
out for baseball, but the captain said to him, "Wilson, you would
make a dandy player, if you were not so . . . lazy." Ill health
forced him to drop out of Davidson and to move to Wilmington
to live with his family.

Upon recuperation he entered Princeton University from
which he later graduated. He was not a "star" student, ranking
forty-first in a class of 122 (not quite in the upper one-third
of his class). He became managing editor of the *Princetonian*
and President of the Athletic Committee. While a student at
Princeton he prepared calling cards saying, "Thomas Woodrow
Wilson, Senator from Virginia." He was best known for his participation in the debating society, but in this society he had
problems, because he would never defend a cause in which he
did not believe.

Upon graduation he continued his studies in law at the University of Virginia. The profession he wanted was politics. The
profession he entered was law. He entered the one because he
thought that it might lead to the other.[2]

After law school he opened a legal practice in Atlanta. Following one year in the practice of law, he gave it up as a profession.
His biographer says of him, "The strong strain of idealism in his
nature was outraged by the materialism and pettiness of everyday legal practice. He was shocked by the sight of two talented

advocates squabbling over a stolen chicken; political preferment seemed to descend upon men like Hoke Smith, already on the road to the United States Senate, whom Wilson considered a mere ambulance chaser. So Wilson abandoned both the law and his hopes for a political career. Instead he would be a professor of political science, content to operate as an 'outside force' in government." [3]

From this experience he continued his education at Johns Hopkins for an advanced degree, and after teaching at Bryn Mawr and Wesleyan he finally accepted a professorship at Princeton. It is interesting that at Wesleyan he also coached football.

As a professor he was unusually popular. Students frequently interrupted his classes with applause. They would line up outside his class to see if some student failed to arrive, in the hope that they might get a seat. Within a short while, he was president at Princeton, then governor of New Jersey, and finally president of the United States.

It is difficult for me to picture Woodrow Wilson as a human being. I can see him as an idealist, as a president, as a prophet. But I have felt that this boyhood hero of mine was "untouchable" until just this week I ran into a volume containing his love letters.

His first wife was Ellen Louise Axson, whose father was pastor of the First Presbyterian Church of Rome, Georgia. During their courtship he wrote her. "You knew that I loved you before I told you, didn't you, love? Why, I had told you often enough by plain enough signs, and even by pretty plain words. Do you remember the verses I gave you as we rode home from a picnic? I remember the charming blush with which you read them, but did not dare interpret it as I wished I might. Did you imagine that I had copied all those lines to give you just because I thought them pretty and hoped they would interest you from a literary point of view?" [4]

Still later he wrote a letter that was so characteristic of a young man in love, "My own darling, I am sick at heart from not hearing from you. It is now a week since you must have reached home and not a line have I had from you. I am filled with apprehensions. . . . I know that there must be some reason, but what can it be? The past week has seemed like a month—I am astonished to find that it is still September." [5]

He had the same problems that most young men have. His beloved's guardian did not think it proper for a young girl to visit in a boy's home. Only after receiving an invitation from Woodrow Wilson's mother was her guardian willing for her to go.

One other letter indicates something of his feeling. "My own darling, I cannot describe to you my delight at the receipt of your letter. I had come away from the post office with a heavy heart so often that . . . when I took your letter from the envelope . . . I was almost frightened at the way my heart beat. It was the sweetest letter ever written—and it seems to have been written with great rhetorical art, for it observed the laws of climax, beginning 'My dear friend' (as if I were nothing more!) and ending with confessions of love which are the sweetest, as well as the most modest that ever a maiden made." [6] How beautifully he expressed his love when he said, "My darling, I am sometimes absolutely frightened at the intensity of my love for you." [7] On another occasion he said, "How can a fellow in Baltimore write a lecture when he is forever thinking of a girl in Georgia?" [8]

Woodrow Wilson was every inch a man, but in a courtship he was able to describe the deep sensitive feelings of a man in love. The test of a man's character is seen clearly in the quality of his love and the nature of his acceptance of responsibility for the emotional, moral, and spiritual health of the woman he loves. It is in our love that we are under the most intensely selfish and self-giving forces that we ever encounter. It is in this very area that a man is most visibly seen to be a man of God, or a man who thinks only of himself.

Woodrow Wilson proved himself in this early relationship of his life.

I have already indicated that he was a very popular professor at Princeton and was recommended by the faculty to be president.

It was quite a shock to students and trustees alike that almost instantaneously he instituted reforms. The first was to change the very nature of the school from a sleepy, finishing school for young men into an institution of academic excellence. He sought to initiate small classes and high standards. One student wrote home to his father, complaining, "Princeton is getting to be nothing but an . . . educational institution." [9]

Two great controversies marked the decade of his administration. He felt that the eating clubs had become centers of snobbery and did not enhance the educational processes. He therefore proposed to do away with these groups and form quadrangles where students would live, eat, talk with their school mates and with single professors. The faculty and trustees accepted this plan, but when the alumni heard about it, they rose up in arms. They were not as interested in an educational institution as in a finishing school.

The second great battle was with Dean West who was extremely popular with certain wealthy patrons. This dean wanted to move the graduate school a distance away from the campus and to have full control of it. Wilson thought that the graduate school should be the center of the campus and under the direct rule of the president. In this battle Wilson was accused of lying. Because of a large multimillion dollar bequest the new graduate center was created. The trustees turned against Wilson and supported Dean West. This was not the first time nor the last that money dictated the policy of a great institution. Those who know the history of the school felt that Wilson was forced to resign, but he saved face because he had been offered the nomination of the Democratic party to be governor of New Jersey.

Wilson's friends felt he would never have accepted the nomination had he not lost in his battle with this dean and the trustees. To my mind this is just another case of God shutting a door that man wanted to enter, so that he would enter another door that God had prepared for him. I am reminded of the words of Joseph when he said to his brothers who had sold him as a slave, "You meant it for evil, but God meant it for good."

Wilson had fought hard for democracy and justice while he was president of Princeton. He was known throughout the state as a great speaker and leader and so was easily elected governor, but as governor of New Jersey he refused to submit himself to the control of the party bosses. "To their dismay he demonstrated a powerful grasp of legislative politics, and overcoming old guard opposition from both parties, he forced passage of one reform bill after another. These established a direct primary, penalties for corrupt corporate practice, greater protection for the working men, controls to regulate railroads and public utilities." [10]

So successful was Wilson in his battle for the rights of man that in 1912 he was nominated by the Democratic party to be its candidate for president of the United States. He had not sought the office. Since the founding days of our republic no candidate had been nominated by a majority party who had made less personal commitments to get the nomination. Although he did not win the majority of popular votes, he won a landslide electoral college victory over the other three candidates.

Big business, having no concern for working conditions or salaries, was running roughshod over labor. Wilson lived in the time that marked the twilight days of the "robber barons."

One of his aims was to attain justice for the laboring man. He initiated the eight-hour day and removed from Interstate Commerce all commodities produced by child labor.

He also brought about currency reform, establishing the Federal Reserve System.

Many people feel that Wilson was naïve in foreign affairs. He was either naïve or whistling in the dark, for in his first annual message to Congress in December 1913, he said, "Many happy manifestations multiply around us of a growing cordiality and sense of unity among the nations, foreshadowing an era of settled peace and good will. . . ."

Almost immediately there was trouble in Mexico, and within a year World War I broke out in Europe. Through all of this he stood for justice for all people, for the right of self-determination for the Mexican people, and for American neutrality in the European War. The newspapers openly called him a coward for not getting into the European War and for not intervening more strongly in Mexico. He made repeated attempts to be the mediating force to stop the war in Europe and to secure from Germany a pledge to stop submarine warfare. On several occasions he was able to get the Germans to stop submarine warfare. In spite of the warmongers who were calling Wilson a coward, the American people re-elected him as their president in 1916.

Because of German submarine warfare that was killing our citizens and ignoring the rights of neutrals, in 1917 Wilson asked Congress to declare war on Germany.

His great dream was peace and not war. He turned the running of the war over to General Pershing and devoted great energy to finding the ways of justice and to restoring peace. He finally issued his Fourteen Points which called for a settlement without total victory and included in the Fourteen Points was the League of Nations. It outlawed war and banded nations together in a total economic, trade, social, and military boycott of any nation that seemed to be creating international trouble. There was to be no telephone service to any nation infringing upon the rights of another nation. It was his feeling that nations should be treated as individuals, and that when they broke the law, society should step in and stop them.

After the armistice of November 11, 1918, Wilson went to Paris to lead in the battle for peace, self-determination, justice for all people, and the League of Nations. He knew that unless they secured justice without recrimination they would be laying the seeds for the continuation of the war. But Clemenceau, Lloyd George, and Orlando of Italy were so interested in acquiring German colonies, in seeking special privileges for their nations, and in stealing everything that they could from the vanquished enemy that they would not hear the real meaning of Wilson's great plan.

In speaking of the Fourteen Points Clemenceau said, "God gave us the ten commandments, and we have broken all of them. Wilson gave us Fourteen Points. We shall see."

This country went through its normal period of wanting to withdraw from the world. We had fought in Europe and were tired of it and wanted to have nothing to do with Europe. Senator Lodge of Massachusetts, the grandfather of Henry Cabot Lodge, led the isolationist battle in the Senate. Senators who had anything against Wilson tried to destroy him by destroying the League of Nations. Everyone who wanted us to live apart from the world joined them in opposition of the League. Sensing that he was going to have to go to the American people rather than the Senate, Wilson started a speaking tour of the country to secure support. In one of his appeals he spoke to those who called him a dreamer, interested in altruistic purposes. "To such appeals," said Wilson, "some gentlemen, who are themselves incapable of altruistic purposes, say, 'Ah, but that is altruistic. It is not our business to take care of the world.' No, but it is our business

to prevent war, and if we do not take care of the weak nations
. . . there will be war." [11]

To those who suggested that the League was giving up sovereignty, he said, "You have heard it said, my fellow citizens, that
we are robbed to some degree of our sovereign, independent
choice by articles of that sort. Every man who makes a choice
to respect the rights of his neighbors deprives himself of absolute
sovereignty, but he does it by promising never to do wrong, and
I cannot for one see anything that robs me of any inherent right
that I ought to retain when I promise that I will do right, when
I promise that I will respect the thing which, being disregarded
and violated, brought on a war in which millions of men lost
their lives, in which the civilization of mankind was in the bal-
ance, in which there was the most outrageous exhibition ever
witnessed in the history of mankind of the rapacity and disregard
for right." [12]

It was on this trip that he suffered a stroke from which he
never recovered.

In speaking of Wilson's failure, Jan Christiaan Smuts said, "It
was not Wilson who failed in Paris. It was humanity."

For his efforts he received the Nobel Peace Prize.

There are those who said that Wilson made mistakes, and he
did. But men who criticize him for his attempts at justice, opportunity, fairness, and peace will have to stand before Almighty God and answer the question of what they did with the
trust that was handed to them. There was a statement in the
Reader's Digest that I think is very pertinent, "We see the hand-
writing on the wall, and all we do is criticize the formation of
the letters."

As a result of this blindness humanity had to suffer the ravages
of a world-wide depression and the Second World War. The
greed, maliciousness, envy, and stubbornness of political leaders
who had been selected to lead us to peace and justice brought
on these catastrophies.

In our day of revolutions on the campuses and in so many of
the nations of our world, we might learn a great deal if we would
read the words of Woodrow Wilson as he wrote about the Russian Revolution:

"What gave rise to the Russian Revolution? The answer can only be that it was the product of a whole social system. It was not . . . a sudden thing. It had been gathering head for several generations. It was due to the systematic denial to the great body of Russians of the rights and privileges which all normal men desire and must have if they are to be contented and within reach of happiness. The lives of the great mass of the Russian people contained no opportunities, but were hemmed in by barriers against which they were constantly flinging their spirits, only to fall back bruised and dispirited. Only the powerful were allowed to secure their rights or even to gain access to the means of material success."

Wilson had this criticism of capitalism: "Have not many fine men who were actuated by the highest principles in every other relationship of life seemed to hold that generosity and humane feeling were not among the imperative mandates of conscience in the conduct of a banking business, or in the development of an industrial or commercial enterprise?

"And, if these offenses against high morality and true citizenship have been frequently observable, are we to say that the blame for the present discontent and turbulence is wholly on the side of those who are in revolt against them? Ought we not, rather, to seek a way to remove ﹆such offenses and make life itself clean for those who will share honorably and cleanly in it? . . .

"The sum of the whole matter is this, that our civilization cannot survive materially unless it be saved only by becoming permeated with the Spirit of Christ and being made free and happy by the practice which springs out of that spirit. Only thus can discontent be driven out and all the shadows lifted from the road ahead. Here is the final challenge to our churches, to our political organizations, and to our capitalists—to everyone who fears God or loves his country. Shall we not all earnestly cooperate to bring in the new day?" [13]

What gave him the courage to stand for love and purity prior to his marriage? What was it that made him stand for the working man against the business empires of America? What made him stand against the banking interest that cared nothing for people? What made him willing to be called coward and to stand for justice in international relations? What was it that caused this man to say, "Even if giving my own life would accomplish this end, I would gladly give it?"

Someone said of Wilson, "He was unseduced by flattery, unawed by opinion, undismayed by disaster. He faced life with antique courage and death with Christian hope."

It has been said that to raise up a man God has to start with his grandfather. Woodrow Wilson's heritage was Christian in every respect. He firmly believed that his God must be the determining force in every decision in his life, and he made Jesus Christ the one great source of idealism and power.

He was always reticent to talk about his spiritual experiences. He would rather practice them. He repeated this incident to some friends, "One time my father was attending a religious meeting when other ministers were relating their religious experience. My father did not join. A minister, turning to him, said, 'Have you no religious experiences, Dr. Wilson?' 'None to speak of,' was the reply." [14]

In speaking of the Bible Wilson once said, "The opinion of the Bible bred in me, not only by the teaching of my home when I was a boy, but also every turn and experience of my life and every step of study, is that it is the one supreme source of revelation, the revelation of the meaning of life, the nature of God and the spiritual nature and need of men. It is the only guide of life which leads the spirit in the way of peace and salvation. If men could but be made to know it intimately, and for what it really is, we should have secured both individual and social regeneration." [15]

Two thousand years ago God sent a man, his own Son, to save the world. The evil within man's heart caused men to crucify him. In our own century, God has raised up another man who could have led us from chaos, war, and depression. This man was not divine, as Jesus was. He was human. Because men were greedy and full of hate, they turned their backs on him.

Society is judged, not by the leaders that God sends, but by its response to that leadership. How much of the chaos of the modern world might have been avoided had the Christian community sought to make their Christian faith an active force, not only within their devotional lives, but in the marketplace where man lives. In conclusion I would remind you of one of Wilson's most significant statements. It comes out of his address when he was inaugurated president of Princeton. "We are not put into the world to sit still and know. We are put here to act."

# Churchill, Moses, and God

$R$ECENTLY I CAME ACROSS one of the most remarkable sermons I have ever read. The author has not taken his own ideas and read them into the Bible but has done an outstanding job of Biblical study incorporated with sound Biblical scholarship.

One remarkable thing about this sermon is that while the author deals with the Biblical character, Moses, even a hasty reading of the sermon shows that it is as truly autobiographical as it is biblical. Quite obviously, the author sees in Moses a man with many of the same challenges that he faces. To read this sermon on Moses enables us to understand the life of its author, whom *Reader's Digest* calls, "The Man of the Century." Winston Churchill in this message bares his own inner soul.

My purpose is not to point you to Winston Churchill. Rather, I would let him point you to one of the greatest men of all history—Moses, and through Moses, to Jesus Christ. This is the aim of Churchill's sermon just as it is the aim of this chapter.

Let me begin by saying that Churchill had a great reverence for the Scriptures. In this sermon he says:

"We may be sure that all these things happened just as they are set out according to Holy Writ. We may believe that they happened to people not so very different from ourselves, and that the impressions those people received were faithfully recorded and have been transmitted across the centuries with far more accuracy than many of the telegraphed accounts we read of the goings-on of today. In the words of a forgotten work of Mr. Gladstone, we read with assurance upon 'The impregnable rock of Holy Scripture.' . . . Let the men of science and of learning expand their knowledge and probe with their researches every detail of the records which have been preserved to us from these dim ages. All they will do is to fortify the grand

simplicity and essential accuracy of the recorded truths which
have lighted so far the pilgrimage of man." [1]

Mr. Churchill had a profound faith in God and felt that God
had tapped him on the shoulder for special work. His secretary,
in writing of him, said: "He seems to have a simple, rather typi-
cally English belief in God—The God of Rudyard Kipling, the
Empire Builders and the country squire. He knows his Bible
well and quotes it frequently. But his choice of quotations is
characteristic: 'Ask, and it shall be given you, . . . knock, and
it shall be opened unto you.' . . . He quotes a God who helps
those who help themselves." [2]

The feeling that God had tapped him on the shoulder developed
early in his life. After having faced what seemed sure death a
number of times, we are told that "Winston's . . . escapes made
him superstitious. He was increasingly certain that he was des-
tined for great events." [3]

As early as 1911 he foresaw the coming struggle with Germany,
and in response to his warnings he was made First Lord of the
Admiralty. On that night he opened his Bible and read from
Deuteronomy: "Understand therefore this day, that the Lord
thy God is He which goeth over before thee, as a consuming fire
He shall destroy them . . . Not for thy righteousness or for the
uprightness of thine heart dost thou go to possess their land;
but for the wickedness of these nations the Lord thy God doth
drive them out from before thee." [4]

Twenty-nine years later, having been made prime minister of
England, in the dark days at the beginning of the war, he wrote:
"As I went to bed at about 3 A.M. I was conscious of a profound
sense of relief. . . . I felt as if I were walking with Destiny [he
spelled Destiny with a capital D], and that all my past life had
been but a preparation for this hour and for this trial." [5]

This profound belief in God was highlighted when at the
close of World War II he appeared before the House of Commons
and offered the following motion: "That this House do now . . .
give humble and reverent thanks to Almighty God for our deliverance from German domination." [6]

Churchill's faith went beyond a belief in God to an acceptance
of and dedication to Jesus Christ. As he brings his sermon on

Moses to a conclusion, he says: "Many centuries were to pass before the God that spake in the burning bush was to manifest himself in a new revelation . . . as the God not only of justice, but of mercy; a God not only of self-preservation and of survival, but of pity, self-sacrifice and ineffable love." [7]

And so the man who believed in the Scripture as the "Impregnable rock," who had a simple belief in God, and who felt that God had called him into high service, wrote for himself, his day, and for posterity a remarkable sermon on Moses. This sermon explains Churchill as well as it explains Moses.

We note in this sermon that God calls people in terms of their basic concerns.

Moses was born of Hebrew parents in a society that did not want him. Pharaoh was plagued by a population explosion among the Hebrew people and ordered that all Hebrew male babies be killed. When Moses was born, his mother made a boat and placed him in it. She then saw to it that the boat floated down the Nile to the place where the daughter of the Pharaoh was bathing. Pharaoh's daughter saw the boat, discovered the baby, and adopted Moses as her own. Even though he was raised in the court of royalty, he never forgot his heritage.

At the end of the first phase of his life, Moses was observing the work that his Hebrew kinsmen were required to do by their Egyptian overlords. Seeing an Egyptian harm one of the Hebrews, he killed the Egyptian. This meant that he had to flee from Egypt, for it only gave further proof to the oppressing Egyptians that one could not trust any Hebrew, even though he was reared in the Royal Palace.

This concern for his people never left him. Years later, after he had brought them out of Egypt, they committed a great sin. It seemed as if God himself would now turn against them and destroy them. Moses pleaded with God and said: "Alas, this people have sinned a great sin; . . . But now, if thou wilt forgive their sin—and if not, blot me, I pray thee, out of thy book which thou hast written." [8]

Moses thus demonstrated his willingness to risk his life and his own personal future for his people. Because of this love for them, God was able to use Moses as their leader. No man can lead for long who does not have a real concern for those whom he has been called to lead. It is this type of concern which God must look for if he would find a leader for his people.

It is this kind of concern which Churchill had for the people of England. As a young man he got his first glimpse of what it meant to live in the slums. A visit to the Manchester slums horrified and fascinated him. He said: "Fancy living in one of these streets, never seeing anything beautiful, never eating anything savory, never saying anything clever!" In 1908 Charles Masterman wrote of him: "He is full of the poor whom he has just discovered. He thinks he is called by Providence to do something for them." [9]

As a result of this he delivered a revolutionary speech saying, "I look forward to the universal establishment of minimum standards of life and labor. We want to draw a line below which we will not allow a person to live and labor, yet above which they may compete with all the strength of their manhood." [10]

It is significant that Churchill phrased his motto: "In war, resolution; in defeat, defiance; in victory, magnanimity; in peace, good will." The concern that led him to fight for the poor made him fight against Germany. He found in Julius Caesar his ideal of a political leader, because Caesar was so generous to defeated enemies.

When God wants a leader, he must choose a man of concern.

A young pastor in Pennsylvania saw a picture of gang life among New York's teen-agers. The pictures moved him to tears. So touched was he that he moved his family to this area and began a work that is so significant that six years later it has a budget of $670,000. His concern is for the socially deprived and the narcotic addicts. *Life* magazine, which ran the series that brought tears to his eyes, later carried a sequel story on what one man's tears and action have done.[11]

Moses' concern led him to a foolish and impetuous act in killing the Egyptian. Churchill's concern led him to switch political parties. Reverend David Wilkerson's concern led him to leave Pennsylvania for the slums of New York. God could take these concerns and use them for his glory.

When God wants a man to do a job, he looks for a person who is concerned. The second command is "Thou shalt love thy neighbor as thyself." "By this shall all men know that ye are my disciples, if ye have love one to another."

It may be that God has not used us because we have not loved enough.

Moses fled Egypt and made his home in the Sinai peninsula. Here he married and became a nomadic herdsman. One day he came upon a bush that seemed to be burning but was not consumed. As he went close, God spoke to him out of this burning bush.

God told Moses that He also was concerned over the plight of the Hebrew people in Egypt, and that He had decided to do something about it. He then told Moses that he, Moses, was to be His instrument for leading the children of Israel out of Egypt and into the Promised Land.

Moses was completely overcome. He still had concern, but he did not believe that he could do the job. God told him that he himself would send the particular power necessary to overcome the Egyptians. He would send the plagues. But still Moses was hesitant. God gave him certain miraculous tricks that he could perform. But still Moses was unsure. He did not feel that he was competent as a spokesman. God assured Moses that He had made Moses' tongue, and also promised him a spokesman. Finally Churchill says, "God was able to convince Moses that He would work miracles through him."

It was in this faith that God would work miracles through him that Moses went back to Egypt and became the great leader of Israel. It is only as people are convinced that God can and will perform miracles through them that they are able to be of ultimate service to God and man.

It has been said that modern humanism is loving but powerless. It believes in loving one's neighbor, but has little faith in a God who will make love effective. Modern fundamentalism has great faith in God, say some, but it has little love for man. Only when love for man and faith in a God who will work miracles through us, only when these are combined is there potential for great leadership. Love and faith are indissolubly bound within the heart that God can call to lead.

It was the Apostle Paul who in the days of the early church best combined these qualities of love and faith. He was able to write that great hymn of love:

"If I speak in the tongues of men and of angels, but have not love, I am a noisy gong or a clanging cymbal. And if I have prophetic powers, and understand all mysteries and all knowledge, and if I have all faith, so as to remove mountains, but have not love, I am nothing. If I give away all I have, and if I deliver my body to be burned, but have not love, I gain nothing. Love is patient and kind; love is not jealous or boastful; it is not arrogant or rude. Love does not insist on its own way; it is not irritable or resentful; it does not rejoice at wrong, but rejoices in the right. Love bears all things, believes all things, hopes all things, endures all things." [12]

But it was also Paul who wrote, "If God is for us, who is against us." He was also able to say, "I can do all things in him, who strengthens me." Was this not what Jesus meant when he said, "He who believes in me will also do the works that I do; and greater works than these will he do, because I go to the father. Whatever you ask in my name, I will do it"?

This type of faith in ultimate triumph gave birth to the "V" sign which symbolized Churchill. Could anyone listen to his speeches without getting that sense of victory over defeat which brought the Western Civilization through its greatest crisis? Read some of those words: "We shall not flag or fail. We shall go on to the end. We shall fight in France, we shall fight in the seas and oceans . . . we shall defend our island whatever the cost may be. We shall fight on the landing grounds, we shall fight in the fields and in the streets, we shall fight in the hills . . . We shall NEVER surrender . . . Even if, which I do not for a moment believe, this island or a large part of it were subjugated and starving, then our empire beyond the seas . . . would carry on the struggle . . . until, in God's good time, the New World, with all its power and might, steps forth to the rescue and liberation of the old." [13]

It is this persistent faith that transforms a well-meaning concern into victorious action. When a man becomes convinced that God can work miracles through him, then the world will know that it is in the process of being transformed. If our faith is as a grain of mustard seed, we shall be able to move mountains.

Leadership in our world depends to a large extent upon our

knowledge that God is with us and behind us. We are not alone, but are his instruments for salvation, for hope, for justice, and for truth.

It would not have been enough for Moses to have been concerned and to have believed. When he died what he did would have died with him. But Moses called upon all who would hear his voice to give themselves in sacrifice for a destiny that was greater than themselves.

Moses' great farewell address to his people says:

"I have set before you this day life and good, death and evil. If you obey the commandments of the Lord your God which I command you this day, . . . then you shall live and multiply, and the Lord your God will bless you in the land which you are entering to take possession of it. But if your heart turns away, and you will not hear . . . I declare to you this day, that you shall perish. . . . I call heaven and earth to witness against you this day, that I have set before you life and death, blessing and curse; therefore choose life, that you and your descendants may live, loving the Lord your God, obeying his voice, and cleaving to him." [14]

His successor Joshua issued a similar call to the people: "Choose this day whom you will serve, whether the gods your fathers served in the region beyond the River, or the gods of the Amorites in whose land you dwell; but as for me and my house, we will serve the Lord." [15]

Do you recall the challenge that Jesus set before his followers? "If any man would come after me, let him deny himself and take up his cross and follow me. For whoever would save his life will lose it, and whoever loses his life for my sake will find it." [16] He makes another radical call to sacrifice when he says, "If anyone comes to me and does not hate his own father and mother and wife and children and brothers and sisters, yes, and even his own life, he cannot be my disciple. Whoever does not bear his own cross and come after me, cannot be my disciple." [17] The ultimate call was uttered when He said, "Seek ye first the kingdom of God." [18]

Winston Churchill unhesitatingly called his people to sacrifice and destiny. "I have nothing to offer but blood, toil, tears and sweat. You ask what is our policy? It is to wage war by sea, land and air, with all our might and with all the strength that God can give us. . . . You ask what is our aim? I can answer in a word; it is victory at all cost, victory in spite of terror, victory, however long and hard the road may be . . ." [19]

Just a few months later, he said: "The whole fury and might of the enemy must very soon be turned on us. Hitler knows that he will have to break us in this island or lose the war. . . . Let us therefore brace ourselves to our duties and so bear ourselves that, if the British Empire and its commonwealth last for a thousand years, men will say: 'This was their finest hour.' " [20]

God's leaders must call upon their people for radical sacrifice: sacrifice in terms of social standing, personal health, family ties, wealth, even their bodies. Is not this the meaning of Romans 12:1-2? "I appeal to you therefore, brethren, by the mercies of God, to present your bodies as a living sacrifice, holy and acceptable to God, which is your spiritual worship. Do not be conformed to this world but be transformed by the renewal of your mind, that you may prove what is the will of God, what is good and acceptable and perfect." It was Paul who heard this call, and answered, "For to me to live is Christ, and to die is gain." [21]

The Communists of our day call upon their people for radical sacrifice. If we fail to call upon those who claim the name of Christ to give their bodies as a living sacrifice, then we have utterly failed in our own calling.

When God needs a job done, he calls upon a person who does not think that he can do it alone. He calls upon a person who is willing to challenge the best in those around him, that through their concerted effort his kingdom may come, his will may be done.

> Like a mighty army
> Moves the Church of God;
> Brothers, we are treading
> Where the saints have trod. [22]

How those words of Arthur Cleveland Coxe ring out:

We are living, we are dwelling
In a grand and awful time,
In an age on ages telling;
To be living is sublime.

Hark the waking up of nations,
Hosts advancing to the fray;
Hark! what soundeth is creation's
Groaning for the latter day.

Sworn to yield, to waver, never;
Consecrated, born again;
Sworn to be Christ's soldiers ever,
O for Christ at least be men!

O let all the soul within you
For the truth's sake go abroad!
Strike! let every nerve and sinew
Tell on ages, tell for God.[23]

When the world is in a crisis, God calls leaders for its salvation. These leaders are his instruments. When the Hebrew people were slaves in Egypt, God laid his hands upon the shoulders of Moses. When Western civilization faced its greatest crises with Germany, God plucked Churchill from out of the crowd.

It is not just great world crises that concern our Heavenly Father. Our own city faces its crises; your business faces them every day. Your family and club move from one crisis to another. God needs a man! This man must have concern, faith, and willingness to challenge the greatest that is in those who are around him.

# Albert Schweitzer

# Reverence for Life

Someone has written; "A saint is a man who makes goodness attractive." If this could be said of any man in our century, then surely it can be said of Albert Schweitzer. One lady put it this way: "The first time he held my hand and looked at me, I felt a power of goodness running into me like an electric current. I have never, before or since, felt anything quite like it." [1]

Another biographer has said of him: "The story of this great man—musician, philosopher and doctor—who rejected a brilliant musical career at its height, to put into practice his philosophy of life, reminds one of the story of St. Francis of Assisi. . . . This man has shown, probably more vividly than any other, that 'No way of life makes more sense than the way taught by Jesus.'" [2]

Albert Schweitzer was born in Germany on January 14, 1875. His father was an evangelical minister. When he was five years old, he started taking piano lessons. At eight he started playing the organ. Before he was thirty, he had a world-wide reputation in philosophy, theology, and organ. At twenty-one he had decided to dedicate the years before his thirtieth birthday to study. He became the head of a theological seminary and pastor of a local church while continuing his studies.

One day he saw an advertisement for missionaries to go to Africa. He decided to study medicine and go as a medical missionary to tropical Africa. To accomplish this he had to enter medical school. He finished his work in medicine and surgery, and in 1913 at the age of thirty-eight he and his bride set out for Africa. He built his own hospital at Lambarene in French Equatorial Africa. When World War I started, he was placed under house arrest by the French, later being transferred to an internment camp in France. After the war he went back to Lambarene, where he died in 1965 at the age of ninety. Albert Schweitzer won the Nobel Peace Prize in 1952 for his service to humanity.

Schweitzer is known for his monumental two-volume work, *The Philosophy of Civilization.* The first volume is entitled *The Decay and Restoration of Civilization,* and the second volume is *Civilization and Ethics.* He is also known for his religious books, some of which I will mention later.

Albert Schweitzer and George Nitschelm walked home together from school and were involved in the same boyhood experiences. One day, as they walked home from school, George said to Albert, "You wouldn't dare to fight me. I'm too strong for you."

"That's what you think," retorted Albert.

"Right!" exclaimed George. "Come into the field and I'll bet you I'll come out the winner."

For a time they sparred, and then all of a sudden the young Schweitzer knocked his opponent off his feet and straddled him across the chest.

"There you are!" he exclaimed. "What do you say now?"

"You win," George gasped, "but if I got good broth for supper twice a week like you do, I'll bet you wouldn't have won."

Albert did not reply. After a brief pause he got off George, stood up, picked up his satchel, and hurried home.

That evening there was broth for supper. As Albert took the plate from his mother, he felt sick. He could hear George Nitschelm's voice saying again, "If I got good broth twice a week as you do, I'll bet you wouldn't have won." He pushed back his plate. "I'm not hungry. May I go to my room, please?" Up in his room he went over again the thoughts which had come to him so suddenly when George had first made his remark, and he came to a decision. He would not be different from the village boys any more. They must be real friends. He refused to wear an overcoat when the weather grew cold because the other boys did not possess overcoats.

The young Schweitzer's sensitivity extended beyond his concern for people. Shortly before his death he wrote: "From childhood, I felt a compassion for animals. Even before I started school I found it impossible to understand why, in my evening prayers, I should pray only for human beings. Consequently, after my mother had prayed with me and had given me a goodnight kiss, I secretly recited another prayer, one that I had composed myself. It went like this, "Dear God, protect and bless all living beings. Keep them from evil and let them sleep in peace."

Schweitzer continues: "An experience I had in my seventh or eighth year made a deep impression on me. My friend, Henry Braesch, and I had made slingshots. It was in spring during Lent that he said to me, 'Let's go up the mountain and shoot birds.' I thought this was a terrible thing to do, but I did not dare object for fear he would laugh at me. We came upon some birds perched upon a tree, still leafless after winter. Without the slightest sign of fear, they sang sweetly into the morning sunshine.

"My friend, crouching like an Indian, put a pebble in his slingshot and took aim. Obeying his look of command, I did the same, but with terrible pangs of conscience. I made a silent vow to miss. At that moment, the sound of church bells began to mingle with the sunshine and the singing of the birds. . . . For me, it was a voice from heaven. I threw aside my slingshot, and fled home. . . . The bells rang into my heart the commandment, 'Thou shalt not kill.' " [3]

Schweitzer tells us how the phrase "Reverence for life" came to him. He was traveling up an African river to visit the sick wife of one of the American missionaries. "Lost in thought, I sat on the deck of the barge, struggling to find the elementary and universal conception of the ethical which I had not discovered in any philosophy. Sheet after sheet I covered with disconnected sentences, merely to keep myself concentrated on the problem. Late on the third day, at the very moment when, at sunset, we were making our way through a herd of hippopotamuses, there flashed upon my mind, unforeseen and unsought, the phrase, 'Reverence for life.' The iron door had yielded; the path in the thicket had become visible. Now I had found my way to the idea in which world-and life-affirmation and ethics are contained side by side!" [4]

---

[3] Adapted from *The World Book Year Book* © 1964 Field Enterprises Educational Corporation.

Each day of Schweitzer's life was dedicated to the maintenance of life. He said, "Good means to maintain life. Evil means to destroy life." [5]

In one of his last messages written for the *World Book Year Book,* 1964, he said: "Compared to former generations, inhumanity has actually grown. Because we possess atomic weapons, the possibility and temptation to destroy life has increased immeasurably. . . . All . . . suggestions thus far have been impotent to create the mutual trust which is necessary. . . . Trust is a matter of the spirit. It can come about only when the spirit of reverence for life rises in all nations. . . . The course of history demands that not only individuals become ethical personalities, but that nations do so as well." [6]

Need I also say that Schweitzer was a man of deep and controlling Christianity. Every morning and evening he conducted prayers for the patients and staff at his hospital. He did not turn the Sunday worship services over to a chaplain but conducted them himself. At one time he served a church as pastor while also being principal of a theological school. During his confinement as an internee of the French during World War I he was allowed the freedom to serve a church in the community where the internment camp was located.

He is described as being as somberly realistic as Jeremiah, as sweeping in his historical judgments as Isaiah, as severe in his condemnation as Amos, as impatient for the kingdom as Daniel, as tender and gracious as Hosea.

It was his reaction against the liberalism that discarded so much of Jesus' teachings that caused him to seek to find out who Jesus really was. This led to his writing *The Quest of the Historical Jesus.* It also forced him to ask whether Jesus was crazy or if he was the most sane man who ever lived. For his doctoral thesis in medicine he wrote *The Psychiatric Study of Jesus.* In an attempt to understand what Jesus meant by "the kingdom of God," he wrote *The Mastery of the Kingdom of God.* He also wrote *Paul and His Interpreters* and the *Mysticism of Paul the Apostle.*

In all of this he was seeking to worship God with his mind. If he was to follow this man, this Messiah, then he felt that he must understand him.

Schweitzer was a preacher who was able to speak simply and

to the heart. He explained the love of God in one of his sermons by saying: "Let me express it in a simile. There is an ocean-cold water without motion. In this ocean, however, is the Gulf Stream, hot water, flowing from the equator toward the Pole. Inquire of all scientists how it is physically imaginable that a stream of hot water flows between the waters of the ocean, which, so to speak, form its banks, the moving within the motionless, the hot within the cold; no scientist can explain it. Similarly there is the love of God within the God of the forces of the universe —one with Him, and yet so totally different. We let ourselves be seized and carried away by that vital stream." [7]

He loved the church, an emotion he inherited from his father. In writing about his father he said, "My father's sermons used to make a great impression on me, because I could see how much of what my father said in the pulpit was of a piece with his own life and experience."

There were churchmen who reacted against Schweitzer's conclusions in his books. But all too often they did not take into account the sterile liberalism and the purile fundamentalism against which he was reacting.

Are you joining in the contemporary quest to understand Jesus and make his life your own? When we apply the test, "By their fruits shall ye know them," then this man of God stands tall in the history of Christian saints.

Note also that Schweitzer was a man of action.

For the last centuries the church has been long on theoretical piety—and short on thoroughgoing practice. It has been sound in theology—and heretical in discipleship. It has loved to hear sermons—but seldom witnessed dedication. It has talked about being saved—but seldom shown that it was saved from sin. If Schweitzer did not understand the words of Jesus, he dug into them. We pass them by for something simpler.

Europeans and Americans who were raised in the last part of the nineteenth century were still smarting under the knowledge that American and European white men had captured, killed, or made slaves of from thirty to fifty million Africans. This would correspond to making slaves out of 15 percent of the living Americans. This had been done with the support of churches and leading churchmen.

The blackness of that guilt is one of the darkest pages in the history of the white man and the Christian movement. Feeling the burden of that guilt, Schweitzer felt that he could fulfill his obligation to Jesus and to Africa most adequately by becoming a missionary doctor.

He went to Africa at the age of thirty-eight to establish his hospital. He had practically no staff and certainly was not treated with the respect due Europe's greatest organist, leading theologian, and outstanding philosopher. The African had lost all faith in white men. As one biographer says, they "accept the medicine and steal the mosquito net when they leave." [8]

On one of his birthdays, Albert Schweitzer said, "Do not congratulate me, rather sympathize with me. I wish I was only thirty. I have so much to do." [9]

It might do us good to remember that Jesus said: "He who believes in me will also do the works that I do; and greater works than these will he do, because I go to the Father."

I am convinced that man can never make up by gifts of money what he has not done with his life. I am also convinced that no amount of listening to sermons, offering prayers, ushering or working in the organized life of the church can make up for the personal commitment of obedience to Jesus and love of man that are required by the gospel. Any saving of the soul which does not issue in sacrificial service to mankind is a heresy far more dangerous than any heresy of the mind.

The story of Lazarus and Dives (Latin, meaning "the rich man") is credited with driving Schweitzer from Europe to Africa:

"There was a rich man, who was clothed in purple and fine linen and who feasted sumptuously every day. And at his gate lay a poor man named Lazarus, full of sores, who desired to be fed with what fell from the rich man's table; moreover the dogs came and licked his sores. The poor man died and was carried by the angels to Abraham's bosom. The rich man also died and was buried; and in Hades, being in torment, he lifted up his eyes, and saw Abraham far off and Lazarus in his bosom. And he called out, 'Father Abraham, have mercy upon me, and send Lazarus to dip the end of his finger in water and cool my tongue; for I am in anguish in this flame.' But Abraham said, 'Son, remember that you in your lifetime received your good things, and Lazarus in like manner evil things; but now he is comforted here, and you are in anguish. And besides all this, between us and you a great chasm has been fixed, in order that those who would pass from here to you may not be able, and none may cross from there to us.' And he said, 'Then I beg you, father, to send him to my father's house, for I have five brothers, so that he may warn them, lest they also come into this place of torment.' But Abraham said, 'They have Moses and the prophets; let them hear them.' And he said, 'No, father Abraham; but if some one goes to them from the dead, they will repent.' He said to him, 'If they do not hear Moses and the prophets, neither will they be convinced if some one should rise from the dead.' " [10]

There are places in our world where you can serve. Are there human beings with needs in our community? Dives, will you continue to ignore them?

Jesus went about preaching, teaching, healing. To those who followed him, he said, "If you believe in me, the works that I do, you will be doing also."

We have all done a lot in our world. Have we done as much as he assigned?

# Helen Keller

# First Lady of Courage

THE STORY OF HELEN KELLER is the story of two lives and not one. Without Anne Sullivan as her teacher and companion, she might never have become the first lady of courage.

To follow the story chronologically, we must begin in Springfield, Massachusetts. Anne and Jimmy Sullivan were the children of an ignorant, alcoholic father. An early case of traucoma caused partial blindness in Anne. The mother's knowledge of medicine was at a level where she sought to cure the disease by bathing the girl's eyes in geranium water. In desperation they sought help through prayer to the Virgin Mary. Her father felt that all his daughter's eyes needed was a drop of water from the blessed River Shannon in Ireland. Not being able to go back to Ireland to get the water and finding that prayers to the Virgin Mary and the geranium water did not cure, Anne was left in blindness.

Her mother died when she was ten years old. At that time there were no places where she could be taken for adoption, no foster homes, and no children's homes where she could be helped. Instead she was sent to the state infirmary where she lived with the social derelicts, the unwanted, the old and the poor. Some of us still remember those county poor farms that are similar to the place where she was taken.

Seventy of the eighty infants received into the home the year before she went there died within the year. In the year when Anne and her brother Jimmy were put into the infirmary, Anne was the only survivor. Cases of d.t.'s, insanity, and contagious disease—young and old—men and women—were all quartered together.

Her deformed brother, Jimmy, died soon after they went to

the Tewksburg home. She says, " 'I crept to the side of his bed and touched him. Under the sheets I felt the little cold body and something in me broke. My screams wakened everyone in the hospital. Someone rushed in and tried to pull me away; but I clutched the little body and held it with all my might. Another person came, and the two separated us. They dragged me back to the ward and tried to put me in bed; but I kicked and scratched and bit them until they dropped me upon the floor, and left me there, a heap of pain beyond words.' She followed her brother to the death house; and the next day to his grave. There was no service, because the priest was sick." [1]

When Anne was fourteen an investigating committee from the state came to look over this poor house. The fourteen-year-old girl tugged on the coat of one of the investigators and said, "I want to go to school." Finding that she was almost blind, he arranged for her to be sent to the Perkins Institution for the Blind at Boston. When she arrived, she did not know how to spell or write her name. She had no toothbrush, petticoat, hat, coat or gloves. She received treatment, kindness, had two operations, and by the time she was twenty she was ready to go to work.

The scene shifts to Tuscumbia, Alabama, on June 27, 1880. Tuscumbia is one of the tri-cities—Florence, Sheffield, and Tuscumbia—on the Tennessee River where our government has built great defense installations. It is very close to Huntsville and the Marshall Space Center.

Arthur Keller was a former captain in the Confederate Army who, after the war, had become a newspaper editor. He had two sons by his first wife, and then married Kate, who was twenty years younger than he.

Kate Keller came from a long line of outstanding people. Among them was Edward Everett, the congressman who gave the first address at Gettysburg on the day on which the president of the United States was ignored and allowed to give only a five-minute talk. Another relative was Edward Everett Hale, author of one of the most famous books published during the Civil War, *The Man without a Country.* She was also a descendant of Alexander Spotswood, an early colonial governor of Virginia, and was a distant cousin of Robert E. Lee. [2]

Arthur and Kate Keller's first child was Helen. Eearly in life she uttered her first word, "water". When Helen was nineteen months old, she developed a fever. The doctor was called. He found no symptoms that he recognized. He gave her medicine that had no visible effect. His final diagnosis was, "She has an acute form of congestion of the stomach . . . and the brain." For many days they were not sure that the child would live. Finally she fell into a peaceful sleep and her fever left her. Her mother spoke to the child while she was still in bed and wondered why she did not reply. She noticed that the child continued to stare at the ceiling. She suddenly realized that the little girl did not see. The hysterical scene surrounding this discovery is vividly portrayed in the magnificent play *The Miracle Worker.*

Upon  realizing that her daughter could neither see nor hear, Mrs. Keller whispered, "Oh, God, she is alone in the dark." [3]

If someone were to ask me which was the greater tragedy—to be deaf or blind—I think that I would reply, blindness. Helen Keller, who suffered both, came to a different conclusion. She wrote: "I am just as deaf as I am blind. The problems of deafness are deeper and more complex, if not more important, than those of blindness. Deafness is a much worse misfortune. For it means the loss of the most vital stimulus—the sound of the voice that brings language, sets thoughts astir, and keeps us in the intellectual company of man." [4]

The primary concern of the family was for her blindness. They took her to the outstanding physicians in the area.

American society has been interested in the blind for less than fifty years. There was very little medical knowledge about blindness. I was amazed as I read the history of our treatment of blindness to find that although there has been a great deal of concern for the blind throughout history, practically nothing was done for the blind in the way of training until the last ten years of the eighteenth century. The first three institutions for the blind were established in 1832 and 1833. During his life, Jesus had shown a great interest in the blind and the deaf, but during its history the church which followed him had seldom gone beyond giving them handouts.

From the time she became blind and deaf until she was six years old, she became a selfish, spoiled, vicious, destructive animal. One author says: "She ran around the room, kicking and making animal sounds and knocking things over. . . . They had not succeeded in teaching Helen any manners and this proved embarrassing, particularly at the dinner table. Helen grabbed her food and stuffed it into her mouth with her hands, like an animal. She often ran around the table, snatching food from other people's dishes and sometimes throwing it on the floor. Most of the time her parents did not protest this behavior, but when they did, Helen always flew into a tantrum." [5]

The climax came right after her little sister, Mildred, was born. Helen found the baby asleep in her own doll cradle. She knocked the cradle over, throwing the baby in the air. Mrs. Keller was able to catch the baby before it hit the floor, saving the baby from serious injury.

Following this incident they took her on a long train trip to see Dr. Chisholm, a prominent oculist in Baltimore. He sent them to Dr. Alexander Graham Bell, inventor of the telephone and teacher of the deaf. Dr. Bell took a personal interest in the little girl, and she responded to him.

Through Dr. Bell contact was made with the Perkins Institution for the Blind in Boston. The director, Dr. Michael Anagnos, agreed to find a teacher to come and live in Tuscumbia and assume responsibility for Helen.

Anne Sullivan, whose childhood we described earlier, seemed a natural to him. She accepted the position and moved to Alabama with the Keller family.

The story of Anne's arrival and early experiences with Helen Keller is one of the most exciting that has come out of human history. When you see it on the stage, or in a film, you are convinced that it must be bad fiction, for no one would write such an account of human behavior. This experience became the center of action for the play *The Miracle Worker*.

It began at the dining room table. Helen's manners were embarrassing and animal-like. With a great deal of reluctance, Helen's parents agreed with Anne's request that they leave the room. Anne locked the doors, and then there was a physical wrestling match on the stage that was a short resumé of kicking, biting, screaming, food throwing, hair pulling that lasted for one entire hour. Finally Anne won, made the wild child pick up her spoon and sit in her chair. She then forced her to eat with the spoon, but Helen was not tamed yet. When Anne indicated that she should fold her napkin and leave it on the table, Helen threw it on the floor. Anne demanded that the napkin be folded and put on the table. Helen kicked, screamed, fought, and wrestled for another hour. Finally she was subdued.

The next day Anne asked permission for the two of them to move to a small house in the backyard of the main house.

In a very few days the magic breakthrough occurred. Anne had been trying to make Helen understand the difference between the words "water" and "mug." They were standing at the pump. The water spilled into the mug, and over Helen's hand. Anne spelled the word "water" into Helen's hand. All at once she knew that the word "water" being spelled in her hand and the word for the cold liquid splashing over her hand were synonymous. On that day Helen Keller discovered that "everything has a name." [6]

Almost immediately she learned the word "teacher"—then "walk," "sit," "run."

From this time on Helen was a new girl. That night as they got into bed together, Helen cuddled close to Anne for the first time since they had met. Anne says it was the most triumphant day in her life. Once the breakthrough had been made, progress was rapid.

The most difficult time in learning was when they moved from concrete objects to abstract ideas. It began with Anne Sullivan spelling into Helen's hand, "I love you, Helen." Here is the story in Miss Keller's words:

" 'What is love?' I asked.

"She drew me closer to her and said, 'It is here,' pointing to my heart, whose beats I was conscious of for the first time. Her words puzzled me very much because I did not then understand anything unless I touched it.

"I smelt the violets in her hand and asked, half in words, half in signs, a question which meant, 'Is love the sweetness of flowers?'

" 'No,' said my teacher.

"Again I thought. The warm sun was shining on us.

" 'Is this not love?' I asked, pointing in the direction from which the heat came. 'Is this not love?'

"It seemed to me that there could be nothing more beatiful than the sun, whose warmth makes all things grow. But Miss

Sullivan shook her head, and I was greatly puzzled and disappointed. I thought it strange that my teacher could not show me love.

"A day or two afterward I was stringing beads of different sizes in symmetrical groups—two large beads, three small ones and so on. I had made many mistakes, and Miss Sullivan had pointed them out again and again with gentle patience. Finally I noticed a very obvious error in the sequence and for an instant I concentrated my attention on the lesson and tried to think how I should have arranged the beads. Miss Sullivan touched my forehead and spelled with decided emphasis, 'Think.'

"In a flash I knew that the word was the name of the process that was going on in my head. This was my first conscious perception of an abstract idea.

"For a long time I was still—I was not thinking of the beads in my lap, but trying to find a meaning for 'love' in the light of this new idea. The sun had been under a cloud all day, and there had been brief showers, but suddenly the sun broke forth in all its southern splendour.

"Again I asked my teacher, 'Is this not love?'

" 'Love is something like the clouds that were in the sky before the sun came out,' she replied. Then in simpler words than these, which at that time I could not have understood, she explained: 'You cannot touch the clouds, you know; you feel the rain and know how glad the flowers and the thirsty earth are to have it after a hot day. You cannot touch love either; but you feel the sweetness that it pours into everything. Without love you would not be happy or want to play.'

"The beautiful truth burst upon my mind—I felt that there were invisible lines stretched between my spirit and the spirit of others." [7]

Finally Anne was able to arrange for Helen to go to the Perkins Institution for the Blind where she still continued to be her teacher but where Helen was able to use the Braille library and other facilities available.

Word quickly got around that a miracle had happened to this girl. John Greenleaf Whittier, Oliver Wendell Holmes, Phillips Brooks—all took an interest in her.

Helen's vocal chords had not been hurt by her illness. Hearing no language she did not know that you could communicate with your mouth. At first they were able to teach her one syllable or one letter. Imagine the difficulty of trying to pronounce properly syllables and words that you had never heard. Her only contact was her ability to feel the effect of speaking on people's throats, lips, and tongues. To try to imitate the forms and vibrations that she felt was her only means of learning to speak. Her intense desire in learning to speak proved her downfall. Her vocal cords had become weak. The first few days after she learned to speak she spoke so loudly that she injured her vocal cords. Those who heard her in later years found her speech difficult to understand.

She was soon able to learn to swim, ride horseback, and even ride a bicycle.

Upon her graduation from preparatory school she applied for admission to Radcliffe College, one of the outstanding women's educational institutions of the world. To no one's amazement she graduated from Radcliffe cum laude. During those years she had written a best selling book about her life, had articles published in *Ladies' Home Journal* and other periodicals.

The difficulties of getting an education according to the classical lines of the late nineteenth century were overwhelming, but she learned English, French, and German. She read the great authors in each of their native languages. Shakespeare was one of her favorites. The books of Ruth and Esther in the Old Testament were greatly loved.

Her most serious difficulty came with algebra and trigonometry. She had much trouble differentiating the signs. Triangles, angles, mathematical symbols caused her many hours of agony. (Let me suggest to any high school or college young person having difficulty with mathematics that he read Helen Keller's description of her difficulties with these subjects.)

Helen Keller and Anne Sullivan were absolutely inseparable. It was long before the days of seeing eye dogs. In her book *The World I Live In,* she described how she could identify by their vibrations things she could not hear. Through vibrations she could hear music, tell what tools were being used, and even differentiate between people by the way they walked.

I had often wondered if she had any romance in her life. She did. Helen became attracted to a writer. They made a secret agreement to be married and applied for a license. A newspaper reporter happened to see Helen Keller's name on the list for a marriage license. The next day the story broke in all of the papers throughout the country. Helen's mother became very angry, told the young man to go away and never come back. He left, having written Helen a letter. They never saw each other again.

Anne Sullivan also had a romance and was married to John Macy. Her close relationship with Helen Keller caused the marriage to end in a permanent separation.

Following her graduation from Radcliffe, Helen Keller devoted herself to writing, public appearances, and work for the blind. For example, she saw to it that one system of the alphabet for the blind was established rather than the five different systems that had previously been used. The American Foundation for the Blind became her special instrument for service.

Prior to the Second World War she made a tour of Japan where blindness is far more prevalent than here. Her trip created new interest in the problems of the blind and gave great hope to those in that country who had suffered as she suffered.

During the World Wars she spent much of her time visiting hospitals and talking to the servicemen who had been blinded or rendered deaf in battle.

On one occasion she delivered a speech to Lions International. So deeply moved were the members of that association that they made care for the blind their international project.

We must not forget that it took a combination of Helen Keller's faith, courage, and ability—and Anne Sullivan's patient determination, courage, and ability to create the Helen Keller that we know. As one newspaper writer said, "It is perhaps worth reminding the readers that the wonderful feat of dragging Helen Keller out of her hopeless darkness was only accomplished by sacrificing for it another woman's whole life, and if ever the attempt is made in a similar case, it must be at the same cost." [8]

Her death occurred quietly on June 1, 1968.

We think that we remember Helen Keller because of her handicaps. Ralph Barton Perry, in his introduction to her life, has said: "It is true that Helen Keller is 'handicapped'—as, indeed, who is not? But that which distinguishes her is not her handicap but the extent to which she has overcome it, and even profited by it. She calls for sympathy and understanding, but not for pity. No one can know her or hear her without feeling admiration and gratitude." [9]

Some of us seem to forget that everybody has troubles. Helen Keller is not remembered for the troubles she had, but for the fact that she did something with them. The Dallas Cowboys would never be remembered for games that they won against a team of six-year-old boys. They will be remembered for their victories over the San Francisco Giants and the Miami Dolphins. Great handicaps can produce great victories.

Perhaps this is what the Lord had in mind when he said, "To him that overcometh, I will give the crown of life."

# Pope John XXIII

# Apostle of Brotherhood

WHEN POPE JOHN learned that Mrs. John Kennedy had arranged an audience with him, he was as anxious as any of us would have been about how to greet her. He did not speak English and did not know how to properly address the wife of the president of the United States.

He learned that the audience was to be carried out in French, as both he and Mrs. Kennedy had great fluency in that language. Pope John inquired as to how he should address her. He was told that he could use either the French "Madame" or the American "Mrs." Neither of these seemed to satisfy him, but he was determined to use Madame."

When the beautiful and vivacious Mrs. Kennedy came into the room and knelt for the audience, Pope John seemed to have been overcome. Instead of addressing her as "Madame," he arose from the papal throne and with arms outstretched said, "Jacqueline."

It is quite remarkable that the man we know as Pope John even lived. Perhaps it is one of the acts of special grace. He was born in Sotto il Monte in northern Italy in 1881, the fourth child in a family of thirteen. He was from a poor family. As he once said, "Italians lose their money through women, gambling, and farming. My family chose the slowest route." [1]

He never forgot his peasant background. He once said, "The representative of the highest spiritual authority of the earth is glad, indeed boasts, of being the son of a humble but robust and honest laborer." [2] Once someone asked Pope John what he would like to do after the Council finished its labors. He replied, "Spend a whole day tilling the fields with my brothers."

Many in the Roman Catholic church feared that infants would

be damned if they were not baptized prior to their death. Because of the high mortality rate in the community, immediately after giving birth to her son, Signora Roncalli and her husband walked to the village church in the rain, carrying their newborn infant. They found that the priest was away and would not be back for a while. They sat and waited in the church as the rain dripped through the ceiling around them. After four hours, the priest arrived, saw the newborn infant, his mother and father, and told them he was too tired for the baptism. They insisted, so he carried out the ceremony, accidentally inverting the two given names. The family then walked back home through the rain, feeling more confident since their infant had been baptized on the day of his birth.

When he was six years old, Angelo Roncalli started to school. He had to walk the mile each day barefooted. The priest who was the teacher had three classes of boys of all ages. His only means of discipline was boxing their ears when they made mistakes. Angelo was not known as a student, but he did read everything that he could find. When he was nine years old, he went to another school three miles away.

One afternoon this peasant boy was walking through the field where his father had been working. The father took his spade, shoved it into the earth repeatedly until its blade shone like silver. The blade was pointed like a bishop's hat. Roncalli looked at his boy and said, "I hope I will live to see the day when you are wearing the hat of a bishop."

Angelo continued his studies and finally decided that he should go to the seminary. After he had been in the seminary for a while, he became sick and greatly discouraged. His parents decided that he should give up his studies and come back and work on the land. Angelo was given a letter by his parents to take to the president of the seminary announcing his withdrawal from the seminary. He read the letter as he was walking, tore it up, and managed to continue his training.[3]

He never considered himself a great theologian or scholar. A large percentage of a pope's statements are prepared for him by his staff. He sent one such statement back for several major revisions, protesting, "It's much too complicated! My faithful surely know that I don't know all that. Write the text over again, more succinctly, more simply, and make it less technical. Above all make it more concrete."[4]

Before the First World War, he served as an assistant to the bishop of Bergamo. In this area the laboring man was treated very poorly. In 1909 a group of factory workers went on strike. Angelo's bishop sent the striking workers money, because he was convinced that their cause was just. The community leaders and the industrial backers were shocked that their bishop would side with labor. The bishop was in a great deal of trouble for his stand until he received the complete backing of the reigning pope.

On the other side of the labor question someone once asked John how many persons worked at the Vatican. His reply was, "Oh, no more than half of them!" [5]

Later he sought to organize the "League of Women Workers" in order to help the women get the same rights as men had. Perhaps some of you did not know that he was one of the early leaders in what we now speak of as "women's lib."

Once when attending a banquet he found himself seated next to an elegant lady in a dress cut generously low at the neck. When dessert was served, he invited her to take an apple from him. When she hesitated, he added, "Do take it, Madam, please do. It was only after Eve ate the apple that she became aware of how little she had on."

During World War I he served first as a medical corpsman, and then as a chaplain. He was in the heart of some of the bitterest fighting that occurred in Italy.

From this experience on, John worked for peace. In 1940 he wrote, "War is a frightful danger. For a Christian who believes in Jesus and His Gospel, it is an iniquity and a contradiction." [6]

Having issued his great encyclical, *Pacem in Terris,* he wrote, "I shall never be able to forget the screams of an Austrian whose chest was torn apart by a bayonet during the war and who was carried to the hospital at Caporetto where I was an attendant. His image became ever more vivid within me as I worked on the encyclical *Pacem in Terris.*"

After the First World War, he started a student house for young men. In this house he gave them beds, listened to their problems, lent them money, and inspired them with his faith and his courage.

Later he was made director of the society for the propagation of the faith and then was sent to Bulgaria to represent the pope in that country. Bulgaria was sharply divided religiously—much

as Ireland is today. On one side was the Bulgarian Orthodox
church, with the power and prestige of the government and leading citizens. On the other side was the small Roman Catholic
minority, who were economically second-class citizens. During
his period in Bulgaria, Angelo Roncalli emphasized that men
must learn to love each other and to work together. He visited
with the poor and the rich. He won the support of all Bulgarian
leadership.

During the Second World War he served in Turkey and
Greece. Again he was an instrument of peace. He served thousands of Jewish people who escaped from Nazi occupied countries. He was instrumental in enabling them to reach neutral
lands.

During his entire life he had sought to be a reconciling force.
One Good Friday he stopped a service in St. Peter's to strike out
a reference to "perfidious Jews" that was made in one of the
prayers.[7]

After the Second World War he was sent as Papal Nuncio to
Paris because so very few Roman Catholic priests were acceptable there. Many of the French people who had fought against
the Nazis felt that the Roman Catholic church and its priests
had capitulated to the Nazis and Adolph Hitler. In a day when
the church was very unpopular in France, Angelo went there
and, as he had done in Bulgaria, Turkey, and Greece, won the
support of the people and their leadership.

In 1953 he was given a diocese, becoming Bishop of Venice.
This was thought to be only a title, for he was well into his
seventies and the Roman Catholic leadership thought they were
honoring an old man who had served the church well. He could
not be content in being a retired bishop. Instead he considered
himself as the priest of the people.

When Pope Pius XII died in 1958, the cardinals of the church
met to secure a successor. Angelo had no idea of being elected
pope himself. He bought a round-trip ticket from Venice to
Rome to participate in the election.

There seems to have been a deadlock among the cardinals as
they voted for the new pope. Finally on the eleventh ballot
Angelo Roncalli was elected the pope.

Those who participated in the election seemed to feel that

they were electing an old man who would live three or four years, holding the office with dignity. They looked upon him as an interim pope. But John was not content with being an interim pope. At seventy-seven he entered the most significant job of his life, and became the most influential pope in recent history, and perhaps one of the outstanding popes in the two thousand years of papacy.

It is the custom that when a man is elected pope the other cardinals approach him, one by one—kneel, kiss his hand, and kiss his foot. Roncalli stopped the first one from kissing his foot, lifted him, embraced him, and gave him the kiss of peace. He saw no reason for maintaining such tradition and ended it then and there.

He chose the name John for himself, because he thought it a gentle name and because his father's name was John, and it was also the name of the church in which he had been baptized.

He quickly broke another custom. It had become traditional that the pope should eat alone. Perhaps no one was considered worthy to share his meals. But John, in keeping with his concept of opening the window and letting the fresh air in, said, "I can't find anything in the Scriptures that says the pope must eat by himself. From now on I'm going to have company when I eat my meals." [8]

John always enjoyed eating, and his figure showed it. He was walking through the streets of Rome and overheard a woman remark to her companion, "God, but he's fat." Pope John turned around and benignly observed: "But Madame, you must know that the conclave (Vatican Council) is not exactly a beauty contest." [9]

The burdens of the office of pope sometimes bothered the man who took the name of John. He once told a visitor that when he found it difficult to sleep that he, Angelo Roncalli, would let John XXIII tell him, "Ah, Angelo, don't make yourself so important, please." [10]

With regard to his infallibility he once said to a group of seminary students, "You know I am not infallible." When they looked surprised, he went on with a smile, "No, the pope is only that when he speaks *ex cathedra,* and I will never speak *ex cathedra.*" [11]

John realized that the church must be brought up to date and must meet the problems of the contemporary world. It was partly out of his desire to bring the church up to date that he called the Vatican Council. As you know such a council is a meeting of the bishops and the cardinals of the church to consider whatever the pope has assigned to them.

Some of those in the inner circles of the church did not want him to call this council. They felt that this should be for his successor to do, and that he, John XXIII, was only an interim pope. When he called the council, one of the men told him that there was not enough time to organize it by 1963. To this John replied, "I meant for it to meet in 1962." And he proceeded with the meeting which began on October 11, 1962.

When asked why he had called the council, he made a gesture toward a window as if to open it, and said, "I expect a little fresh air from it. . . . We must shake off the imperial dust that has accumulated on the throne of St. Peter since Constantine."

John loved the church. He described himself and the church as a water fountain. On one occasion he said, "People of all kinds come to my poor fountain. My function is to give drink to all. To leave a good impression behind, even in the heart of a brigand, seems to me to be a work of love that in due season will bring forth a blessing. The church is not an archeological museum, but the ancient fountain which slakes the thirst of the generation of today as she did that of the generations of the past." [12]

One of the other purposes of the council was to bring about Christian unity. His last words before he became unconscious were, "May they be one."

He once said, "Our duty is to work, even against all hope, for the union of Christians. We are all guilty, and we Latins, I mean we Latins in the East, have had and still have our share of responsibility. If we do not make efforts to disregard our own convenience and to look far beyond ourselves, our decline will proceed at the same tempo as that of the Orientals.

"We shall not hold a historical trial. We shall not seek to know who was right and who was wrong. The responsibilities are shared. We shall say simply, 'Let us reunite, let us put an end to the dissensions.' " [13]

To bring the church up to date, to bring about reunion—these were two of his goals, but the third we mentioned earlier was world peace. I would like to recommend to you his encyclical *Pacem in Terris*. It would make a marvelous study guide for a series of class discussions which would last for several quarters. In it he sounds like Thomas Jefferson in the Declaration of Independence, and yet goes into much greater detail regarding the relationships between men, relations of states to each other, concepts of rights, duties, justice, charity, and freedom.

John was no prophet of doom. At the opening meeting of the Vatican Council on October 11, 1962, he said, "In the daily exercise of our pastoral office our ears are shocked, much to our regret, by the voices of persons who, though burning with religious zeal, are not endowed with too much sense of discretion and measure. In these modern times they can see nothing but calamities and ruin. They say that our era, in comparison with past eras, is getting worse, and they behave as though they have learned nothing from history, which is the teacher of life. We feel we must declare our total disagreement with these prophets of doom who always foretell catastrophes as though the world were close to its end."

John was not afraid to die, but he thoroughly enjoyed life. During an audience of people, he once said, "We will pray for you, for your families. And do you also pray for your Pope. For, to be frank, permit me to tell you that I wish to live a long time. I love life." [14]

After he had been told he had an incurable disease, he said, "I feel in my body the beginning of a certain disturbance which must be natural for an old man. I endure it in peace, even if sometimes it is a little painful, and even if I fear its aggravation. It is not pleasant to think about it, but once more I am ready for everything." [15]

Two days before his death in the midst of great physical sufferings, he said to one of his associates, "Dear Professor, don't be disturbed. My bags are always packed. When the moment to depart arrives, I won't lose any time." [16]

One of his most profound remarks was, "We are entering our eighty-second year. Shall we finish it? All days are good for being born, all days are good for dying." [17]

In studying this man's life, several points have been outstanding in my own mind. The first of these is that a man can rise above his economic, social, and educational background.

When I hear people talking about the fact that they can't do anything better, I shall be reminded from henceforth of John XXIII. No man had a less promising background. Few, if any American citizens, come out of more abject poverty or privation.

If God could enable Angelo Roncalli to become somebody, then we have little excuse.

In the second place, I would share Pope John's commitment to the renewal of the church. He faced much more serious obstacles of tradition than we ever face. But he sought to open the window, let the fresh air in to blow the dust that had accumulated since the time of Constantine. This is no time for us to go back to the Reformation. We must join him in going back to Jesus Christ.

The renewal of the church must be accompanied by bringing the church up to date. This does not mean compromising convictions. It means very definitely putting first-century Christianity into the language of the twenty-first century.

Our forefathers had great difficulty when they translated the Bible from Latin to English. Many of them were killed in this attempt.

We must follow in their footsteps by seeing to it that religion is in the language of this day. If the incarnation means anything it means that God would speak to people in the language of contemporary life.

Last Friday night I participated in a program at the Dallas Municipal Auditorium where the Dallas Symphony and a group of young people presented the rock opera *Jesus Christ, Superstar*.

What thrilled me was that long before the day of the opera all ten thousand tickets had been sold. Young people had paid to come to the Municipal Auditorium to hear about Jesus in their language.

I could find some theological weaknesses in the presentation, but I also find some theological weakness in the ethereal presentation of Jesus as drawn by my friend, Warner Sallman.

We have a marvelous choir in this church. Twice a year the choir and the Dallas Symphony perform some great musical composition. For this presentation we may have 350 persons who want to hear the Christian faith as interpreted by Bach, Schubert, Handel. There are about 350 people in this church who like Bach, Schubert, Handel. We are delighted for them to hear it.

But let no one be critical when ten thousand young people

who are avid fans of rock music want Jesus presented in their idiom!

I only wish that it had been done in this church!

John worked for justice. He supported his bishop when the bishop sided with striking workers. He worked with the early women's lib movement. He helped Jews escape from Hitler. He managed wage raises for the staff at the Vatican. He gave Africans positions of prominence within the church. Everything that he touched ended with people being treated a bit more fairly and responsibly.

The great dream of his life was to be an instrument of peace. His experience in the First World War, his suffering through the Second World War brought about a commitment to the Prince of Peace which has seldom been seen in any church leader. He recognized that peace had to be based upon justice.

He sought for unity of the church. He said that the Vatican Council would not be a trial to find out who was wrong but an invitation of love.

I do seek renewal, but beyond renewal I seek for us to quit focusing our attention on the weaknesses of others and seek to learn to work together in unity and harmony with all those who call Jesus Christ Lord and Savior.

Pope John used his power. A play has recently been published depicting a man who was elected pope, but quickly resigned because he was too Christian to be pope. Every decision that had to be made involved gray areas where if he did the best he could, he knew he would be compromising his highest standards. Therefore, rather than doing the best he could, he abdicated his position as pope. He refused to be involved in anything that was less than perfect.

John practiced love. In reading his diary, *The Journal of a Soul*, I was fascinated by a group of sixty maxims which he drew up while still a seminarian. These maxims became the guiding feature of his life. The first six are as follows:

1. I love thee as I am loved by thee (cf. Romans 13:10).
2. Love is the fulfilling of the law (Ibid.).
3. The aim of our charge is love (I Timothy 1:5).
4. Beloved, let us love one another, for love is of God (1 John 4:7).
5. Show me thy charity and give me thy love.

6. I will love thee, O Lord, my strength and my refuge (cf. Psalm 17:2-3).[18]

Equally interesting among the maxims is the last one:

60. There is no labour where one loves, or if there is, the labour itself is loved (St. Augustine).[19]

Dwight L. Moody once heard the statement that the "world had yet to see what could happen to a life that was totally committed to Jesus Christ." Perhaps we have yet to see this, but I think we get a close approximation of it in John XXIII. I am reminded of my Lord when he said, "By this all men will know that you are my disciples, if you have love for one another."

# Richard E. Byrd

# A Man of Courage and Faith

CHRISTOPHER COLUMBUS, Marco Polo, and Ferdinand Magellan were the great explorers of the Old World. In the first half of this century no man approaches the grandeur of Admiral Richard E. Byrd in the field of exploration.

Byrd was a son of Virginia, arising from one of the great families of that state. There were three brothers—Tom, Dick, and Harry. For years it seemed as if Harry would be the most famous. Had he not been a southerner, Senator Harry Flood Byrd might well have been president of the United States. Richard graduated from Annapolis and served during World War I. He had been in charge of our air force in Canada, and as such he knew the serious problems of weather. He knew that weather not only controlled flying, but made the difference between profit and loss for the farmer. Weather affected industry, shipping, and almost every other phase of life. He was further convinced that you could not understand weather until you understood the polar regions.

In order to begin the understanding of the Arctic region, he arranged for an expedition to Greenland, establishing a base close to what is now Thule. Being assured that one could fly the northern route, in 1926 he flew over the North Pole accompanied by Floyd Bennett.

Aviation was his great love. He believed that man must ultimately learn to fly the Atlantic and that the true conquest of the Atlantic involved taking passengers and freight in a nonstop flight from New York to Paris. In 1927 he determined to test this possibility, and with three other men he set out for Paris four months after Lindbergh had made his solo flight. When he reached the French coast, fog and clouds obscured the country-

side. He approached the area of Paris but could see nothing in
the fog. In desperation he turned back toward the sea and saw
what appeared to him to be a lighthouse. With gas running out
he ditched the plane in the Atlantic Ocean. He had difficulty
convincing the French people that they had just flown in from
the United States. But once convinced, the French made heroes
of them.

He felt that his pioneering work had just begun. Many men
would have considered their work completed with two such
great accomplishments. In 1929 he fulfilled a third dream—one
that won for him the title of "Admiral of the ends of the earth."
He flew over the South Pole.

His first expedition to the South Pole started in 1928 and
lasted until 1930. He established Little America at the Bay of
Whales at the edge of the Ross Ice Shelf. In 1933 he led a second
expedition to the South Pole. It was on this second expedition
that he himself established the Bolling Advance Base in which
he lived for four months alone in the Antarctic night. He
returned on several other occasions heading American expedi-
tions. On March 11, 1957, he died. Dr. Melville Bell Grosvenor
of *National Geographic* fame said of him, "Your whole life
exemplifies the highest ideals of America. All America loves
you." [1]

One of the first questions raised by a life like that of Admiral
Byrd is, why did he do it? What would motivate a man to risk
his life on so many hazardous journeys of exploration? One of
his associates, in speaking of a particular phase of the exploration, said, "It is to no purpose . . . to discuss the use of
knowledge; man wants to know and when he ceases to be
curious, he is no longer man." [2] Byrd himself was introducing a
new explorer to the Antarctic. " 'Well, George, what do you think
of it?' I shall never forget my reply, or the admiral's response to
it. I said, 'Well, Admiral, it's a lot of ice. But what good is it?'
Admiral Byrd turned on his heel and walked away. He didn't
speak to me for two weeks." [3] The desire to know was so
basic within Byrd that he refused to discuss the virtue of knowledge as against ignorance.

On other occasions he made it abundantly clear that he believed that knowledge would enrich the life of men. He was
convinced that we could learn about weather, currents, tides,

the sun, the nature of the space around the earth, the nature of magnetism, and certain facts about life itself if we understood what happens at the Poles. He gave himself to seeking this knowledge even as a man involved in medical research gives himself to the understanding of the nature of the human body and the diseases that affect it.

The particular phase of Byrd's life to which I would introduce you is that period on his second journey to Antarctica when he stayed alone at the Bolling Advance Weather Station, 123 miles south of Little America.

One of the primary questions is: why did he stay alone? We must remember that in 1933 electronic instruments were not available that could record temperature and wind and send that information to another base. If information was secured on weather, a man had to be there to read the thermometer and wind gauges. But why did he go?

The hut which was placed in the ice at the weather station was built for three men. It was the original plan that three men should spend the six months together. This was not possible, because there was not enough time to carry adequate food and supplies for three men. Byrd realized that it was impractical for two men to try to live together for that period of time. Byrd felt that it was too much of a strain on the emotional life of the men involved to have two men live together this long. "Hating or being hated by a man whom you couldn't avoid would be a degrading experience leaving the mark of Cain in the heart. Feeling as strongly as I did, I certainly couldn't ask two other men to do what I wouldn't risk myself. It had to be one man, and that one myself, if for no other reason than that here again I could not bring myself to ask a subordinate to take the job." [4]

Admiral Byrd's desire to go to the weather station alone had another side. His cousin D. Harold Byrd says that even before he went to the Antarctic, he had said that he might stay at the weather station alone. In his book Richard Byrd says that "in the hullabaloo the thinking man is driven to ponder where he is being blown and to long desperately for some quiet place where he can reason undisturbed and take inventory." [5]

He experienced other longings which many of us feel. He says, "I should have time to catch up, to study and think and listen to the phonograph; and, for maybe seven months, remote from all but the simplest distractions, I should be able to live exactly as I choose, obedient to no necessities but those imposed by wind and night and cold, and to no man's laws but my own." 6

When Byrd came back to civilization, he was amazed to find the rumor that had circulated about his stay at the Advance Weather Station. There was a story circulating that he had been exiled by his own men. Another said that he had gone off because of an alcoholic problem, and he wanted to do some serious drinking. He would like very much to have disregarded public opinion, but he learned that to disregard what others think of you is a luxury most of us cannot afford. "What people think about you is not supposed to matter much, so long as you yourself know where the truth lies; but I have found out, as have others who move in and out of newspaper headlines, that on occasion it can matter a good deal." 7

Before he left Little America he gave the following order, "Every man in this camp has a right to be treated fairly and squarely, and the officers are requested to hold this fact in mind. In a sense our status is primitive. . . . We have no class distinctions as in civilization. What a man is back home does not count at Little America. He who may have failed back there has his chance to make good here; and he will not be judged by the position he holds so much as by the way he plays the game and does his job, however humble it may be. . . ." The cook laughingly said to the Admiral, "Remember, no class distinctions at Advance Base!" 8

Before Byrd moved the equipment to the Advance Station, they detected trouble with the ventilation system on the oil heater. They thought the trouble was repaired.

When we speak of Admiral Byrd being left alone, we mean alone in the fullest sense of the word. It was Antarctic night. Temperature in its winter drops down to one hundred degrees below zero. The wind blows from twenty to fifty miles an hour. It was absolutely impossible during the Antarctic night for any vehicle to make the trip from Little America to the Advance Base, or for a plane to fly in. Although radio was coming into its own, they were not able to equip him with voice radio. They could speak verbally to him from Little America, but he had to use Morse code to communicate with them. This was to be done at regular intervals on Sunday, Tuesday, and Thursday at ten o'clock in the morning. At the other times there was no communication. Enough oil and food had been supplied, but it must be remembered that at these temperatures rubber boots become as cast iron, kerosene freezes, flashlight batteries refuse to operate. Even in his hut it took as much as five days for a piece of meat to thaw out. The temperature of the ice packed around the hut was minus sixty degrees.

Almost immediately upon being left alone, he discovered that two essential items had been misplaced. The first was a cookbook. He recalled having cooked bacon and eggs and having made a stew. But he knew nothing about cooking. One of the amusing stories that he tells is the Corn Meal Incident:

"I have only to close my eyes to witness again the succession of culinary disasters. Into a boiler I dumped what seemed a moderate quantity of meal, added a little water, and stood it on the stove to boil. That simple formula gave birth to a Hydra-headed monster. The stuff began to swell and dry up, swell and dry up, with fearful blowing and sucking noises. All innocently, I added water, more water, and still more water. Whereupon the boiler erupted like Vesuvius. All the pots and pans within reach couldn't begin to contain the corn meal that overflowed. It oozed over the stove. It spattered the ceiling. It covered me from head to foot. If I hadn't acted resolutely, I might have been drowned in corn meal. Seizing the container in my mittened hands, I rushed it to the door and hurled it far into the food tunnel. There it continued to give off deadly golden lava until the cold finally stilled the crater." [9]

He adds, "My first jelly dessert bounced like a rubber ball under my knife; the flapjacks had to be scraped from the pan with a chisel." It is interesting to note that in 1957 when a similar Advance Base was having trouble preparing cakes without having them fall, they radioed to Little America. Little America radioed back to the United States, and they received directions directly from Pillsbury Company in this country telling them how to mix the cake so that it would not fall.

They had not packed an alarm clock. This would seem unimportant, but have you ever tried to keep time when you live through six months of total darkness? To set your inner clocks so that you can wake up for an eight o'clock reading of thermometers, barometers, wind gauges is not simple.

Byrd had time for thinking. After two weeks he was able to write down his maturing thought.

"The day was dying, the night being born—but with great peace. Here were the imponderable processes and forces of the cosmos, harmonious and soundless. Harmony, that was it! That was what came out of the silence—a gentle rhythm, the strain of a perfect chord, the music of the spheres, perhaps.

"It was enough to catch that rhythm momentarily to be myself a part of it. In that instant I could feel no doubt of man's oneness with the universe. The conviction came that the rhythm was too orderly, too harmonious, too perfect to be a product of blind chance—that, therefore, there must be purpose in the whole and that man was part of that whole and not an accidental offshoot. It was a feeling that transcended reason; that went to the heart of man's despair and found it groundless. The universe was a cosmos, not a chaos; man was as rightfully a part of that cosmos as were the day and night." [10]

He quickly learned that certain disciplines must be carried out. To preserve his self-respect, he bathed regularly, bathing one third of his body each day. To maintain some level of sociability he read while he ate. He tried to wash dishes in the length of time it took his Victrola to play one record. He took fifteen minutes of exercise each morning. Once a day he went out for a walk in the cold Antarctic weather.

It was on one of these walks that tragedy struck.

He had been fearful of tragedy. He knew that in this life man must always remain alert. But he also knew that we become hardened to danger, and after repeated experiences with it we become careless. This explains many of our physical and moral falls. He wrote, "The tolerable quality of a dangerous existence is the fact that the human mind cannot remain continuously sensitive to anything. Repetition's dulling impact sees to that. The threat of sudden death can scare a man for only so long; then he dismisses it as he might a mealymouthed beggar." [11]

And yet, he became careless himself. When he went for a walk he would take a bundle of bamboo sticks, and each three steps he would drive a stick in the ground so that he would be able to follow it back to the base. In the snow and wind it is impossible to see more than a few feet from you. One day as he was walking, he suddenly realized that he had not been putting out his sticks. He turned and tried to see the last stick he had put into the ground, but he could see nothing. He remembered the direction that the wind had hit his face when he left the base, so he tried to go in the opposite direction for one hundred paces. There he put down a stick and then moved thirty paces in each direction from the stick. After several attempts, he was confident that he was lost. On the twenty-ninth step in one direction he sighted a bamboo stick and was saved.

On another occasion while he was walking, his weight broke through the ice, and the lower half of his body fell into a crevice. He looked into a bottomless pit. He was able to hold on and finally dragged himself out.

On a third occasion he went out of his hut in the midst of a blizzard. The door became frozen shut. He said, "Panic took me then, I must confess. Reason fled. I clawed at the three-foot square of timber like a madman. I beat on it with my fists, trying to shake the snow loose; and, when that did no good, I lay flat on my belly and pulled until my hands went weak from cold and weariness. Then I crooked my elbow, put my face down, and said over and over again, You damn fool, you damn fool. Here for weeks I had been defending myself against the danger of being penned inside the shack; instead, I was now locked out: and nothing could be worse, especially since I had only a wool parka and pants under my windproofs. Just two feet below was sanctuary—warmth, food, tools, all the means of survival. All these things were an arm's length away, but I was powerless to reach them." [12]

Again it was almost a miracle, for he found a discarded shovel that enabled him to get back into his hut.

During this period he summed up his philosophy with the following words, "I am finding that life here has become largely a life of the mind. Unhurried reflection is a sort of companion. Yes, solitude is greater than I anticipated. My sense of values is changing, and many things which before were in solution in my mind now seem to be crystallizing. I am better able to tell what in the world is wheat for me and what is chaff. In fact, my definition of success itself is changing. Just lately my views about man and his place in the cosmic scheme have begun to run something like this:

"If I had never seen a watch and should see one for the first time, I should be sure its hands were moving according to some plan and not at random. Nor does it seem any more reasonable for me to conceive that the precision and order of the universe is the product of blind chance. This whole concept is summed up in the word harmony. For those who seek it, there is inexhaustible evidence of an all-pervading intelligence.

"The human race, my intuition tells me, is not outside the cosmic process and is not an accident. It is as much a part of the universe as the trees, the mountains, the aurora, and the stars. My reason approves this; and the findings of science, as I see them, point in the same direction. And, since man is part of the cosmos and subject to its law, I see no reason to doubt that these same natural laws operate in the psychological as well as in the physical sphere and that their operation is manifest in the working of the consciousness. . . .

"The things that mankind has tested and found right make for harmony and progress—or peace; and the things it has found wrong hinder progress and make for discord. The right things lead to rational behavior—such as the substitution of reason for force—so to freedom. The wrong things lead to brute force and slavery.

"But the peace I describe is not passive. It must be won. Real peace comes from struggle that involves such things as effort, discipline, enthusiasm. This is also the way to strength. An inactive peace may lead to sensuality and flabbiness, which are discordant. It is often necessary to fight to lessen discord. This is the paradox." [13]

Byrd came to realize that there are certain values that must be considered primary. He expresses them so beautifully when he says, "At the end only two things really matter to a man, regardless of who he is; and they are the affection and understanding of his family. Anything and everything else he creates are insubstantial; they are ships given over to the mercy of the winds and tides of prejudice. But the family is an everlasting anchorage, a quiet harbor where a man's ships can be left to swing to the moorings of pride and loyalty." [14]

The great catastrophe was slow in building up. At first there were periods of depression, and then depression and nausea. He realized it was carbon monoxide poisoning. He rebuilt the stove and his other equipment, but he kept getting sicker and sicker. It was during the early period of his sickness that he gave so much thought to the relation of the body and the mind. It was his determination that the body should not control the mind, but rather that the mind should control the body.

"Reason tells me that I have no right to be depressed. My progress in eliminating the indefinable irritants has been better than I expected. I seem to be learning how to keep my thought and feelings on an even keel. . . . Therefore, I suspect that my dark moods come from something affecting my physical being—possibly fumes from the stove, the lantern, or the gasoline generator. If that be the case, then my state of mind may possibly have helped to offset the depressing consequences of the poisoning—if that is what is affecting me. . . . How much resistance, then, can my mind impart to the body if the mind is properly directed?

"Possibly something is harming me physically, and I am making things worse by some negative subconscious emotion. Then my mind and body are both sick, and I have a vicious circle to break. Do the mind and the body exist separately, along parallel lines? Is the physical part mostly mental, or the mind mostly physical? How much does the mental control the physical? Indeed, how much division is there between mind and body? The body can take charge of the mind, but isn't it natural and best for the mind to take charge of the body?" [15]

It was after this that he realized that his chances were slim— that he was dying of poison. He was so sick he was not able to operate the radio effectively. He would not endanger the lives of men by allowing them to come and rescue him. Knowing that it was carbon monoxide poisoning, he kept his stove going only three hours a day, and ice covered the inside wall and ceilings. When he would knock over a liquid, it would freeze to the table. His vomit froze on the floor. On several occasions he lapsed into a coma.

During this experience he says that he was not afraid of death itself. "It was a terrible anxiety over the consequences to those at home if I failed to return. I had done a damnable thing in going to Advance Base, I told myself." [16]

He knew that he had created financial obligations for the trip, that he was letting down his family and the men who were waiting at Little America.

He met his emotional problems with this statement of his faith: "About 3 o'clock on the morning of June 2nd, I had another lucid phase." He reached for his paper and wrote in his diary:

"The universe is not dead. Therefore, there is an Intelligence there, and it is all pervading. At least one purpose, possibly the major purpose, of that Intelligence is the achievement of universal harmony.

"Striving—in the right direction for Peace . . . as well as the achievement of it, is the result of accord with that Intelligence.

"It is desirable to effect that accord.

"The human race, then, is not alone in the universe. Though I am cut off from human beings, I am not alone.

"For untold ages man has felt an awareness of that Intelligence. Belief in it is the one point where all religions agree. It has been called by many names. Many call it God." [17]

In trying to analyze his condition he knew that there would be no help from the outside—that little could be done to improve the ventilation in his shack. He said:

"These are the facts. To the degree that a man is superior to his destiny, I should be able to rise above them. . . . I recognize a big difference between the mere affirmation of faith and its effective implementation. To desire harmony or peace, or whatever word you care to give to the sense of identification with the orderly processes of life, would be a step in the right direction; but this by itself was not enough. I had to work for it. Above everything else, what I sought must be logical—it must be brought about by following the laws of nature. It didn't occur to me to formulate a prayer. I would express whatever urge to pray I had in action—besides, the sheer hunger to live was prayer enough." [18]

For the next two months he barely lived until a rescue party finally reached him. When they found him he was so sick that they could not move him for two more months. They stayed with him, gave him warmth, food, and medical treatment.

Several ideas stand out in my mind. It is superfluous to write about the courage of this man. Anyone who reads the book *Alone,* which is the description of the days at the Advance Station, is well aware of the caliber and content of Byrd's faith in God. We are apt to forget that it was not naked courage but a faith coupled with a sense of responsibility for family and friends that kept this man alive.

Our own generation may be spending entirely too much time indulging itself in the question, "who am I?" while at the same time failing to ask, "what are my responsibilites?" Am I fulfilling the role for which God and life have prepared me? Am I making the most of my time, my brains, and my energy; and in the crises of my life, am I letting down those who had every right to trust and believe in me? These are the type of questions that a real man asks. These were the concerns that put backbone into Richard E. Byrd.

This hero challenges and inspires us. Richard E. Byrd lived as a man ought to live—fought as a man ought to fight—faced death as a man—accepted the challenge of his day—believed in God—and put his faith to work.

# Ralph McGill

# A Newspaperman Who

# Kept His Faith

NEWSMEN HAVE BEEN among the most maligned public servants. They are caricatured as irresponsible, hard drinking, chain-smoking men who are after stories and who care nothing for the truth. When any one of us makes a mistake in a speech, our immediate cry is that we are misquoted, suggesting that these men are false witnesses.

The newspaper business has produced some of the great leaders of our country. Among the great newspapermen one stands out in our generation as being a man in whom God's spirit has dwelt, and through whom God has witnessed. That man is Ralph Emerson McGill, a newsman and former publisher of the *Atlanta Constitution*. Upon his death on February 3, 1969, Billy Graham said, "The death of Ralph McGill will not only be a loss to Georgia and the South, but to the entire nation. His influence went far beyond the South. He was a courageous pioneer in race relations and social reform. Mr. McGill had a great understanding of the Christian faith and had among his friends many clergymen. There is a sense of personal loss on my part because he was my personal friend for twenty years. Many times I called on him for advice and counsel. America truly has lost one of its greatest citizens." [1]

Roman Catholic Archbishop Thomas A. Donnelian said, "Ralph McGill represented everything that was great and good in the South. His passing makes us poorer but his life was such a bright example that it has instilled in us a desire to continue his mission of peace and justice for all God's children. We mourn him, but we are richer that he has lived among us and touched all of our lives." [2]

President Nixon, with whom McGill took a trip to Moscow a few years ago, issued this statement, "There is a kind of courage which not only calls forth praise from friends, but also elicits respect from adversaries. It was this kind of courage, intellectual and moral, which distinguished Ralph McGill. Proud of the deepest traditions of his Southern heritage, loyal to the concepts of integrity and honor which are the pride of his region, he brought to journalism a sense of responsibility and a devotion to truth. His high intelligence and deep sense of compassion made an indelible impression on all who knew him." [3]

It fascinated me that in the article on his death published in his own paper, the *Atlanta Constitution*, the first person quoted was not a president of the United States, a political figure, but an old "wino" who had mooched the price of a bed and meal from Mr. McGill many times. He spent his last fifteen cents for a sympathy card that he wanted delivered to Mrs. McGill and Ralph, Jr.

They went on to quote Julia Johnson, a waitress who served Mr. McGill at a downtown restaurant many times before her retirement. She called the newspaper office, and weeping said, "Trouble has taken this place! What will we do? How will we manage without him?" [4]

Ralph McGill was born near Soddy, Tennessee, on February 6, 1898. When people would ask him where Soddy was, he would say, "Just a few miles east of Daisy, and everyone knows where Daisy is." It is just east of Chattanooga. His family were staunch Presbyterians. Unless you have lived in the Appalachians, you really don't understand the meaning of Scots Presbyterian. They are a courageous, committed, determined, puritanical group of Christians. When he was six years old the family moved to Chattanooga, and there they joined the Central Presbyterian Church. He attended McCallie School in Chattanooga, one of the finest prep schools in existence.

He went to Vanderbilt University and started to take a pre-med course because he did not know anything else he wanted to do. While at Vanderbilt he was suspended from school during the spring of his senior year because he had "sent out phoney

invitations to a bunch of rough necks to attend a prom at what
he considered a stuffed shirt fraternity house."

In reading over his biography I see no mention of Vanderbilt
ever giving him a degree. Other schools made up for that de-
ficiency. He received honorary degrees from Harvard, Notre
Dame, Columbia, Brown, Emory, and twelve other universities.
Upon being relieved of his responsibility at Vanderbilt he went
to the *Nashville Banner.* He also served in the U. S. Marines
during the First World War.

In 1929 he went to Atlanta to work with Ed Danforth in the
sports department of the *Atlanta Constitution.* It was a great
period for sports in Atlanta with Ralph McGill, Ed Danforth,
and Morgan Blake writing the sports columns. McGill eventually
became editor of the *Atlanta Constitution* and then finally publisher. A few years ago his first wife died. Later he remarried.
In Atlanta he was a member of the Episcopal church, a member
of the vestry, and one of the outstanding leaders of Christian
forces in the Southeast.

McGill had several qualities that singled him out as a man
of unique spirituality.

One story out of McGill's life came as a shock to me. Anyone
who knows Georgia politics knows that Ralph McGill and Eugene
Talmadge were among the bitterest enemies in the Southeast.
McGill stood for justice for all people, while Talmadge was never
known as having any sense of humanitarianism or justice. They
made no secret of their political antagonism. In spite of being
at opposite political poles, the two remained friends and McGill
visited Talmadge when Talmadge was dying. Talmadge shocked
McGill by asking him to write his biography. McGill said that
he was flabbergasted, to which Talmadge replied, "My wife and
I have talked it over, and we want you to do it." Talmadge knew
that in spite of their political enmity he would be treated fairly
and with understanding by McGill.

Any time we take a stand in life we are sure to end up with
enemies. Would it not be great if our enemies knew us to be so
fair and responsible that they would choose us to write their
biographies? Based on what you say in your conversations, do
you think your friends or your enemies could trust their lives
and their reputations in your hands? McGill's bitterest enemy

was sure that he could trust his reputation in McGill's hands.

In this connection I would like to say that most of us who speak in public are treated more fairly by the press than we treat them. A recent event illustrates this. At the death of Martin Luther King, Jr. one of our public officials was quoted widely for his remark. He later said that the press had misquoted him. In response to this the press simply played a tape of this official's remarks. They had reported his remark exactly as he made it. Every time one of us says that we have been misquoted when we have not, we are bearing false witness. It may be an easy way out of a difficult situation, but a commandment of God listed among the ten says, "Thou shall not bear false witness." I am the first to confess that it is easy to pass the buck for our responsibility to someone else. When this means breaking one of the Ten Commandments, it assumes a very serious role. Would you break one of the Ten Commandments just to save your own reputation?

McGill represented the integrity and fairness of the press. I can only wish that his opponents would be as fair to him.

McGill believed in law and the Constitution of the United States. He felt that all of us were safe in the hands of the Constitution. In 1959 he won the Pulitzer prize for his editorials. It was his belief in law that got him in trouble with so many southern people. In the mid-fifties it was not popular to believe in law and the Constitution or to have respect for government. Had McGill not come out so strongly for the Constitution and the law he could have been a hero to many who hated him. The editorial that was cited by the Pulitzer Prize Committee was written immediately following the bombing of the Jewish temple in Atlanta. A group of racists wanted to destroy the temple. This was one of the occasions that brought McGill and me together. It was my privilege to invite the temple to have their services in Druid Hills Presbyterian Church where I was pastor until such a time as the temple could be restored. In his editorial McGill said:

"Let us face the facts. This is a harvest. It is the crop of things sown. It is the harvest of defiance of courts and the encouragement of citizens to defy law on the part of many Southern politicians. . . . It will be quite a job for some editors, columnists, and commentators, who have been saying that our courts have no jurisdiction and that the people should refuse to accept their authority, not to deplore. It is not possible to preach lawlessness and restrict it. To be sure, none said go bomb a Jewish temple or a school. But let it be understood that when leadership in high places in any degree fails to support constituted authority, it opens the gates to all those who wish to take law into their hands. There will be, surely, the customary act of the careful drawing aside of skirts on the part of those in high places. 'How awful,' they will exclaim. 'How terrible. Something must be done.' . . . This too is a harvest of those so-called Christian ministers who have chosen to preach hate instead of compassion. Let them find pious words and raise their hands in deploring the bombing of a synagogue. You . . . encourage hatred for the Negro and hope to restrict it to that field. It is an old, old story. It is one repeated over and over again in history. When the wolves of hate are loosed on one people, no one is safe. Hate and lawlessness by those who lead . . . encourage the crazed and neurotic who print and distribute the hate pamphlets—who shrieked Franklin Roosevelt was a Jew—who denounced the Supreme Court as being Communist and controlled by Jewish influences." [5]

It is shocking to me today that many of the people who are shouting the loudest for law and order were shouting their severest repudiations of law in 1954 and 1955. In speaking of the need to have respect for authority McGill said in another editorial, "If these reckless opportunists ever succeed in destroying public confidence in any one branch of our government they then destroy themselves and representative government along with it.

"In the last half of the twentieth century it was no longer possible for the courts of this land to say it was constitutional to discriminate against any American citizen. We are either citizens or we are not. To hold a strongly dissenting opinion to this statement and to voice it is an undisputed right. But to cry it down with reckless attacks on the integrity of our court is dangerous and unpardonable." [6]

In reading over the stories concerning McGill's death, it was not surprising to me that he died in the home of a Negro music teacher with whom he and Mrs. McGill had just had their evening dinner. Mr. John Lawhorn was a music consultant for the State Department of Education. McGill had watched the young Negro educator enchant a group of second grade children with an imaginative music lesson. Lawhorn believed that through music children could improve their vocabulary, their enunciation, their reading skills. Mr. Lawhorn was seeking $6,000. Just before he was struck with a heart attack Mr. McGill said, "Don't let this project die." And then he said he thought he had some suggestions as to how this money could be raised. Mr. Lawhorn never heard the suggestions.

Having been reared in a coal mining town, McGill was well aware of the plight of the people. During the depression days of the 30s he made tour after tour of the depressed farm areas of the Southeast.

In his battle against the economic conditions that produced *God's Little Acre* and *Tobacco Row,* McGill alienated many of the wealthy who wanted to keep their tenant farmers in their place. He fought for equal schools not just for the blacks, but for the coal miners, tenant farmers, cotton mill workers. The southern taxpayer did not want to be taxed for equal schools. He was either able to send his children to private schools or he saw to it that there was a good school in his neighborhood.

It was for those who were oppressed that McGill took his stand. He believed that when the Bible said that Jesus had come to set free those who were oppressed, that it was talking in modern terms, as well as ancient.

One of his closest friends in the newspaper business was one of the columnists for his paper, Celestine Sibley. She has some of the same zeal and convictions that marked the life of her boss. In her article about Ralph McGill's death Celestine Sibley said this: "We were both accredited to cover the trial of James Earl Ray in Memphis. Seats for the press were limited and the *Constitution* was assigned one to be shared by Mr. McGill and me. He would be writing for a world-wide audience in his syndicated column. I would be writing the news story for our paper. When the word came that we had one seat between us he made the inevitable joke about who would sit in whose lap, but then he told me quite seriously that mine was the greater responsibility.

" 'I'll take your place when you have to go to the ladies' room,' he promised me. 'You're the reporter.' " [7]

I am reminded of the Biblical statement that suggests that we count others as more worthy than ourselves.

In 1924 the Presbyterian church in Soddy, Tennessee, had a resident membership of seventy. I don't know how many members it had when McGill was there but probably no more than this number. But I have become acquainted with people all over the Southeast who were in some way related to or else came from the Presbyterian church in Soddy. All of them had deep Christian convictions and had the courage that made them fight for those convictions.

Ivan Allen, the great mayor of Atlanta, spoke of McGill as being the conscience of the South. He never saw himself as a liberal, but rather he said, "I am a conservative fellow with a mortgage and old fashioned Presbyterian conscience." [8]

*The Montgomery Advertizer* said that McGill reminded them of Winston Churchill during the 30s when Churchill "fought to awaken his country to the dangers of a resurgent German war machine. Churchill stood almost alone in his warnings of the Hitler Menace and was denounced as an alarmist and warmonger. He never compromised and, of course, events vindicated him. He said the pain and rejection he endured left him more persuaded than ever that the only course of action—the only policy —for a man of principle was to act each day according to the dictates of his conscience, whatever the consequences." [9]

He led off each day's editorials with a headline and the following question, "How are you prepared to treat your fellow man today, Mister?" Does this not remind you of Jesus' statement, "Inasmuch as ye have done it unto one of the least of these, ye have done it unto me"?

I shall never forget visiting with Ralph McGill in his office. We had talked of mutual concerns. He had told me how some people had thrown rotten eggs at his house; how others stood at the bus stop where he got off to throw decayed food at him; of how the Ku Klux Klan had burned crosses in the front of his home. I don't remember his exact words, but they went something like this, "I am really not a liberal, nor a conservative. I am trying to live my life as God would have me live it. You see this old desk here? (And he pointed to the desk at which he was sitting.) This is the desk of Henry Grady, whom I consider to be the greatest of our southern newspaper editors. I use this desk so that it will remind me of my heritage. I was born and educated in the South. When God called me to be a newspaper man, he gave me a call as definite as your call to the ministry. I love people. I do not like to make enemies. I try to make friends of my enemies. But friends or enemies I am to be a witness to God and to the faith that you and I profess."

I would have two epitaphs for this man. The first would say, "He loved his fellow man." The second would be, "Well done, good and faithful servant."

This is what the Holy Spirit can do with a life turned over to him. It is not important that a Christian involve himself in a church vocation. It is important that every churchman make his vocation an expression of his Christian faith.

# Dag Hammarskjöld

# An Instrument of Peace

Dag Hammarskjöld summed up his philosophy of life when he wrote: "From generations of soldiers and government officials on my father's side I inherited a belief that no life was more satisfactory than one of selfless service to your country or humanity. . . . From scholars and clergymen on my mother's side I inherited a belief that, in the very radical sense of the Gospels, all men were equals as children of God." [1]

At Hammarskjöld's funeral Adlai Stevenson voiced the sentiments of a large part of humanity when he said: "In his passing the community of nations has lost one of the greatest servants it ever had—a brilliant mind, a brave and compassionate spirit. I doubt if any living man has done more to further the search for a world in which men solve their problems by peaceful means and not by force than this gallant friend of us all . . . the very embodiment of the international civil servant." [2]

Philip Toynbee put it another way affirming that Hammarskjöld was the greatest statesman and was "best matched to his hour since Abraham Lincoln." [3]

Hammarskjöld was born on July 29, 1905, and given the name of Dag, which means "the light of day." The name certainly proved prophetic.

His father before him was an outstanding public servant. During his life he served as a professor of law, as Sweden's minister of justice, minister of education, ambassador to Denmark, and other significant positions.

Among his boyhood associates was the family of Archbishop Nathan Soderblom. Soderblom was one of the founders of the ecumenical movement leading to the World Council of Churches.

In his later life when Hammarskjöld was introduced to the general secretary of the World Council of Churches, the secretary asked him if he wanted to know something about the ecumenical movement. His reply was, "Oh, I know all about that. I was brought up under Soderblom." [4]

When he was a young man his family moved to Copenhagen where his father was ambassador and then back to Uppsala, Sweden, where his father was governor of the province. Dag was the fourth son in the family. It is said that the mother had wanted a daughter, rather than a son, and that Dag became her "stay-at-home-daughter," for it was the custom in Sweden that one daughter would not get married and stay with the parents to look after them in their old age. He was very closely attached to his mother and had tremendous respect for his father. Some have suggested that these attachments kept him from ever being married.

During the First World War, Dag's father became prime minister of Sweden. He was an impartial man and refused to join any political party, standing above the politics of his own country. During that war there was a great division in Sweden. His father became the target for political attacks from both major parties as they tried to force Sweden into the war. Woodrow Wilson faced this same problem in the United States prior to our entry into World War I. Dag was too young to understand the issues, but cruel jokes were made about him in school. He was ostracized by his friends. Day after day he went home from school with the jeers of his friends ringing in his ears. In 1917 his father was forced to resign and returned to Uppsala as governor of that province.

In 1920 Albert Schweitzer came to Uppsala to give a series of lectures and concerts. While Dag did not meet Schweitzer in person, he heard him and became fascinated. Describing his own faith, Dag expresses his dependence on Schweitzer, saying: "The two ideals which dominated my childhood world met me fully harmonized and adjusted to the demands of our world of today in the ethics of Albert Schweitzer, where the ideal of service is supported by and supports the basic attitude to man set forth in the Gospels. In his work I also found a key for modern man to the world of the Gospels." [5] Gustaf Aulen in his book, *Dag Hammarskjöld's White Book: The Meaning of Markings,* has a fascinating chapter on Hammarskjöld's dependence on Schweitzer.

Hammarskjöld was an honor graduate of the University of Uppsala and very quickly made his way in service for the government. He prepared an outstanding report on the cycles of inflation and depression as related to the Wall Street crash of 1929 and the subsequent economic problems of the world. As a result of his studies he was given authority in Sweden to try to deal with the problems of the depression and moved to secretary of the government owned bank in Sweden. He continued his service through the Second World War.

Having suffered with his father over the demise of the League of Nations, he was excited and hopeful when the United Nations was founded. He felt that the world could not afford another war and that man's need was not for victory but for peace. Lord Caradon of England backed up this theme in an article in *Vista* magazine (a magazine of the United Nations Association) in August of 1971, saying that mankind needed success in working for peace, rather than victories of pride or aggression for individual nations.

The first paragraph of the charter of the United Nations struck home to Hammarskjöld's heart.

> We, the Peoples of the United Nations, Determined
> to save succeeding generations from the scourge of war,
>     which twice in our lifetime has brought untold sorrow to
>     mankind, and
> to reaffirm faith in fundamental human rights, in the dignity
>     and worth of the human person, in the equal rights of
>     men and women and of nations large and small, and
> to establish conditions under which justice and respect for
>     the obligations arising from treaties and other sources of
>     international law can be maintained, and
> to promote social progress and better standards of life in
>     larger freedom. . . .

In 1953 he was elected general secretary of the United Nations. He had already dealt with the Russians in some very firm and dramatic ways, but was practically unknown in the United States. When France proposed him for what Trygve Lie had called "the world's most impossible job," our delegation had to send word back to Washington asking who Dag Hammarskjöld was, and whether or not they should support him. The reply came back from Washington, "Get Hammarskjöld appointed." [6]

On April 10, 1953, Dag Hammarskjöld took his place as United Nations Secretary. When the first rumor came to him that he was going to be offered the job, he said, "No one has been crazy enough to ask me, nor am I crazy that I would take such a job." But when confronted with the issue, he said, "I must take it, difficult though it is. It is my duty." [7]

His first great controversy was with the United States government. This was during the heyday of Senator Joseph McCarthy. McCarthy had aroused the fear of the American people that certain employees of the United Nations were Communists and wanted them investigated by the FBI. Under pressure from the American government, Trygve Lie allowed the FBI to come into the United Nations to conduct an investigation.

Hammarskjöld reversed this order, saying that the United Nations was an international organization, and that as such he would not allow the Russian government to investigate the pro-American leanings of United Nations employees, and in a similar way he would not allow the American government to investigate pro-Russian leanings of its employees. He regarded every member of his staff as "de-nationalized."

While we respect this position today, it brought him into serious conflict with our government.

In 1955 he opened the Atoms For Peace Conference in Geneva. He had instigated this conference, hoping that the best brains of mankind could be used to aid men instead of to kill them. It was his dream that nuclear energy could generate power for homes, business, and community, and that perhaps it could be used for irrigation, turning deserts into farmlands, and thus feeding the billions of people of the earth.

The mid-fifties brought the Arab-Israeli quarrel to a feverish pitch. It was Hammarskjöld's personal diplomacy that secured this region and brought about a cease-fire by stationing United Nations troops there to protect the right of both Arabs and Jews. This peace was maintained until U Thant withdrew the United Nations troops.

One of his most significant triumphs came as an aftermath of the Korean War when eleven American pilots were taken prisoners by the Chinese Communists who tried them as spies. Tension was mounting between the United States and China, and there were demands in this country for forceful action.

Hammarskjöld visited Red China's prime minister, Chou En-lai. They discussed the issues for four days. There was no obvious result from the meeting until Dag's next birthday (his fiftieth) when Chou En-lai released the American prisoners as a present for Hammarskjöld's fiftieth birthday.

An unknown when he was elected for the first time, he quickly became known as the servant of peace and was re-elected unanimously for a second term in 1958.

Perhaps the greatest crisis that he dealt with was the Congo situation. Belgium had controlled the Congo for years, and then without adequate preparation, suddenly gave freedom to the Congo in 1960. There was an immediate struggle for power with Russia backing one of the groups in the Congo, seeking to establish a communistic regime. In order to bring peace to the Congo, Dag Hammarskjöld led the United Nations and its forces into the Congo, saying, "The only way to keep the cold war out of the Congo is to keep the UN in the Congo." [8] On a recent visit to what was then the Democratique Republic of Congo (now called Zaire), I repeatedly heard Hammarskjöld referred to as the man who saved the country from the Communistic nations.

It was while on a mission to the Congo that Dag's plane crashed, and he was killed.

As we turn to look at his faith, perhaps the best statement that we have concerning the roots of this man's life, is one that he gave to Edward R. Murrow, when Murrow was preparing a series of articles entitled *This I Believe*. Hammarskjöld summed up his life philosophy with these words:

"The world in which I grew up was dominated by principles and ideals of a time far from ours and, as it may seem, far removed from the problems facing a man in the middle of the twentieth century. However, my way has not meant a departure from those ideals. On the contrary, I have been led to an understanding of their validity also for our world of today. Thus, a never abandoned effort frankly and squarely to build up a personal belief in the light of experience and honest thinking has led me in a circle; I

now recognize and endorse, unreservedly, those very beliefs
which were once handed down to me.

"From generations of soldiers and government officials on
my father's side I inherited a belief that no life was more satisfactory than one of selfless service to your country or humanity.
This service required a sacrifice of all personal interests, but
likewise the courage to stand up unflinchingly for your convictions.

"From scholars and clergymen on my mother's side I inherited
a belief that, in the very radical sense of the Gospels, all men
were equals as children of God, and should be met and treated
by us as our masters in God.

"Faith is a state of the mind and the soul. In this sense we can
understand the words of the Spanish mystic, St. John of the
Cross: 'Faith is the union of God with the soul.' The language
of religion is a set of formulas which register a basic spiritual
experience. It must not be regarded as describing, in terms to
be defined by philosophy, the reality which is accessible to our
senses and which we can analyse with the tools of logic. I was
late in understanding what this meant. When I finally reached
that point, the beliefs in which I was once brought up and which,
in fact, had given my life direction even while my intellect still
challenged their validity, were recognized by me as mine in
their own right and by my free choice. I feel that I can endorse
those convictions without any compromise with the demands of
that intellectual honesty which is the very key to maturity of
mind." [9]

"But the explanation of how man should live a life of active
social service in full harmony with himself as a member of the
community of the spirit, I found in the writings of those great
medieval mystics for whom self-surrender had been the way to
self realization, and who in 'singleness of mind' and 'inwardness'
had found strength to say yes to every demand which the needs
of their neighbors made them face, and to say yes also to every
fate life had in store for them when they followed the call of
duty, as they understood it. Love—that much misused and mis-
interpreted word—for them meant simply an overflowing of the
strength with which they felt themselves filled when living in
true self-oblivion. And this love found natural expressions in
an unhesitant fulfillment of duty and in an unreserved accep-

tance of life, whatever it brought them personally of toil, suffering—or happiness.

"I know that their discoveries about the laws of inner life and of action have not lost their significance." [10]

Perhaps one of the most beautiful of his meditations expresses his faith so well.

"Thou who art over us,
Thou who art one of us,
Thou who *art*—
Also within us,
May all see Thee—in me also,
May I prepare the way for Thee,
May I thank Thee for all that shall fall to my lot,
May I also not forget the needs of others,
Keep me in Thy love
As Thou wouldest that all should be kept in mine.
May everything in this my being be directed to Thy glory
And may I never despair.
For I am under Thy hand,
And in Thee is all power and goodness.

"Give me a pure heart—that I may see Thee,
A humble heart, that I may hear Thee
A heart of love—that I may serve Thee,
A heart of faith—that I may abide in Thee." [1]

Dag Hammarskjöld had no fear of death. In fact, there seems to be a preoccupation with it throughout his book *Markings* where he says:

"Do not seek death. Death will find you. But seek the road which makes death a fulfillment.

"Your body must become familiar with its death—in all its possible forms and degrees—as a self-evident, imminent, and emotionally neutral step on the way towards the goal you have found worthy of your life.

"As an element in the sacrifice, death is a fulfillment, but more often it is a degradation, and it is never an elevation.

"No choice is uninfluenced by the way in which the personality regards its destiny, and the body its death. In the last analysis, it is our conception of death which decides our answers to all the questions that life puts to us. That is why it requires its proper place and time—if need be, with right of precedence. Hence, too, the necessity of preparing for it." [12]

His humility and commitment are evidenced by another of his meditations:

> "Have mercy
> Upon us.
> Have mercy
> Upon our efforts,
> That we,
> Before Thee,
> In love and in faith,
> Righteousness and humility,
> May follow Thee
> With self-denial, steadfastness, and courage,
> And meet Thee
> In the silence.
>
> "Give us
> A pure heart
> That we may see Thee,
> A humble heart
> That we may hear Thee,
> A heart of love
> That we may serve Thee,
> A heart of faith
> That we may live Thee,
>
> "Thou
> Whom I do not know
> But Whose I am.

"Thou
Whom I do not comprehend
But Who hast dedicated me
To my fate
Thou—" [14]

On Christmas eve 1960 he recalled and wrote the following words:

Strive, the pains of death endure,
Peace eternal to secure:
For the faithful and the tried
Heaven's Gates shall open wide.[14]
    (Archbishop J. O. Wallin, 1819)

As winner of the Nobel Peace Price, Hammarskjöld stood out as a follower of the Prince of Peace and gave himself that the vision of the Prince of Peace might become a reality in the life of this world.

Just four months before his death, he put what is probably the most significant entry in his diary. "I don't know Who—or what —put the question, I don't know when it was put. I don't even remember answering. But at some moment I did answer *Yes* to Someone—or Something—and from that hour I was certain that existence is meaningful and that, therefore, my life, in self-surrender, had a goal. From that moment I have known what it means 'not to look back,' and 'to take no thought for the morrow.' " [15]

# Dietrich Bonhoeffer

# The Secret of Freedom

Dietrich Bonhoeffer will go down in history as one of the most exciting, courageous, far-sighted martyrs of the twentieth century. Like Albert Einstein, Edward Teller, Enrico Fermi, Erik Erickson, and hundreds of other European giants, he fled Adoph Hitler in the late thirties and escaped to America. Then under the influence of a profound Christian conscience he returned to Germany in the summer of 1939 to join in the opposition of Adolph Hitler, resulting in a martyr's death in April of 1945, just three weeks before Hitler himself committed suicide.

Dietrich Bonhoeffer was born on February 4, 1906, in Breslau, Germany. His father was a noted psychiatrist; his mother was a German house frau who cared for the family of four daughters and four sons. Dietrich was one of twins, his sister being named Sabine. When he was six years old, his family moved to Berlin, living in one of the finer sections of the city, being close neighbors to one of the great theologians and teachers of the century, Adolph von Harnack.

The First World War began when Dietrich was eight years old. During the war one of his brothers was killed, another seriously wounded, and three of his cousins were also killed. The sufferings of the First World War, when combined with the propaganda machine of Kaiser Wilhelm, created hatred in many German hearts toward the United States and Great Britain. In fact it is said of Dietrich that he "liked neither England nor America until they had proved their worth." [1]

He attended the best of schools and suffered less during the harsh years of Germany's privation and starvation than most. He was aware of an annuity policy for twenty-five thousand dollars that his father had purchased before the war, planning to use it for retirement. When the annuity matured in the late twenties, his father cashed it, hoping that it would buy a bottle of good wine and a box of strawberries. When he got to the store the twenty-five thousand dollars would not cover the wine, just the strawberries.[2]

What happened to the Bonhoeffer home was true of all the homes. His father being a noted psychiatrist associated with a group of men who stimulated his children in unique ways. For example, one friend was Max Planck, one of the greatest scientists of his generation. Adolph Von Harnack, whom I have mentioned, Theodore Huess, and others were among his acquaintances.[3]

As a young man he became noted as a scholar, and at seventeen he was ready for Tübingen University. After entering the university he went to Rome where he first had intimate creative contact with the Roman Catholic church, its traditions, pomp, ceremony, and magnificent music. He then went back to the university where he studied under Harnack. Later he became strongly influenced by Karl Barth.

Upon completion of his theological training he went to Spain as an assistant pastor in the German Lutheran church at Barcelona. There he proved so popular that the senior minister would not announce who was going to preach on the next Sunday, knowing that if it was announced that Bonhoeffer would preach the church would be full, and if the senior minister was preaching it would not be full.

It was in Spain that the figure of Don Quixote became indelibly impressed upon Bonhoeffer's mind. In Don Quixote he saw the image of a church inadequately prepared to meet the demands of the modern world.

In July 1930 when Bonhoeffer was twenty-four he became a teacher in the University of Berlin. Before undertaking this teaching assignment he accepted a post-doctoral fellowship at Union Theological Seminary in New York City. In the United States he became particularly interested in the church's involvement in society. He saw our race problem firsthand in Harlem and on a tour he made through the United States. He had little respect for American theology but a profound respect for the way the American church was seeking to put its theology to practice in everyday life.

When he left Germany the Nazi party was just coming into

power. Upon his return Hitler had become the most powerful individual in Germany. About a year after Bonhoeffer's return to Germany he became involved in the ecumenical movement. Speaking of this movement at a conference in Scandinavia, he said, "They have no anchorage in theology to enable them to withstand the waves surging all around them." [4]

He came to realize that hyphened Christianity was inadequate, and that American-Christianity, French-Christianity, German-Christianity must give way to Christianity.

It was during this period also that he went to England to serve a German-speaking church, and he became associated with the Bishop of Chichester, G. K. A. Bell. This further involved him in the ecumenical movement and gave him a contact with Anthony Eden.

Adolph Hitler appointed his own bishop for the Lutheran church and changed church law to make it impossible for a Jew to become a member of the Christian church in Germany. Bonhoeffer and other leaders in the German church saw the dangers of the cult of Hitlerism and the unchristian nature of local congregations which excluded people of Jewish racial stock.

Finally, under great pressure they were forced to found what became known as the Confessional Church of Germany where the only prerequisite for membership was confessing Jesus Christ as Lord. They rejected any concept of racial exclusion.

It was during these years that Hitler forbade Bonhoeffer to publish any of his writings or to preach.

As the pressure mounted, he and others like him were forced into silence and many of them into submission.

Following Hitler's march into Czechoslovakia, Bonhoeffer joined the other European refugees who had fled to the United States. He accepted a lectureship at Union Seminary in New York City. His American friends felt that they were saving him from certain imprisonment and death. Almost immediately he felt he had made a mistake, and so on June 20 he wrote to Reinhold Niebuhr, "I have come to the conclusion that I have made a mistake in coming to America. I must live through this difficult period of our national history with the Christian people of Germany. I will have no right to participate in the reconstruction of Christian life in Germany after the war if I do not share the trials of this same time with my people." [5]

Henry Smith Leiper, then secretary of the Federal Council of Churches, had collected several thousand dollars to bring Bonhoeffer to the states, compared him with Jesus "who had long centuries ago taken the road to Golgotha as he 'set his face steadfastly toward Jerusalem.'" [6] In July of 1939 he returned to Germany after only two months in the United States.

As a young man he had been greatly influenced by Gandhi. His grandmother set aside money for him to take a trip to India to visit Gandhi. Bonhoeffer was never able to make the trip but was particularly attracted by Gandhi's nonresistance and pacifism.

When Bonhoeffer returned to Germany, he felt that he would have to join the underground resistance to Adolph Hitler, and this meant political action. He said, "It is not only my task to look after the victims of madmen who drive a motorcar in a crowded street, but to do all in my power to stop their driving at all." [7]

All of us desire to be righteous and innocent of sin. His faith finally led him to the conviction that he would not only have to join political resistance to Hitler but would find it necessary to participate in the movement to assassinate him.

This went against the grain of his Christian commitment that he should not kill. But the concept of stopping the madman remained a dominant thought in his mind. In his battle with his own conscience he was finally able to say of those who choose innocence above responsibility, "He sets his own personal innocence above his responsibility for men, and he is blind to the more irredeemable guilt which he incurs precisely in this; he is blind also to the fact that real innocence shows itself precisely in a man's entering into the fellowship of guilt for the sake of other men. . . . From what has just been said it emerges that the structure of responsible action includes both readiness to accept guilt and freedom." [8]

His family position, plus his position as a member of the faculty of the University of Berlin, gave him close contact with those men in the German hierarchy who were opposed to Hitler.

Responsible men in the government and the army sought to overthrow Hitler. Bonhoeffer met with these men, and during the early years of the war they devised a plan to overthrow Hitler. But they needed assurance that if they did overthrow Hitler and sued for peace, the Allies would accept the new German government and establish peaceful relationships with the Germans.

Bonhoeffer escaped from Germany, met Bishop Bell of Chichester in Scandinavia, and presented the proposal of the German leadership to him. The Bishop of Chichester immediately went to London and submitted the proposal to Anthony Eden, British Secretary of State for Foreign Affairs.

The Allied leadership rejected this overture and demanded unconditional surrender. Liddell Hart speaks of this as one of the great blunders "that proved of profit only to Stalin—by opening the way for Communist domination of central Europe."

The word of this plot was conveyed to Hitler, and the leadership of the revolutionary forces was put in prison. Bonhoeffer ended up in Tegel prison in Berlin.

It was from the jail that he wrote his influential letters and papers. He joined with the Apostle Paul, John Bunyan, and Martin Luther King whose significant contributions to Christian literature came from jail cells.

Finally he was removed from Berlin to Buchenwald. On April 8, 1945, he was transferred to Flossenbürg. He and others who participated in the plotting of Hitler's death were hanged on direct orders from Himmler. Only three weeks later Hitler himself committed suicide. On the same day Bonhoeffer's brother-in-law, Hans von Dohnanyi, was killed. Klaus Bonhoeffer and his sister's husband, Rudiger Schleicher, were also murdered.

The doctor who witnessed the execution says that Bonhoeffer knelt in his cell, "praying fervently" before removing his prison garb. M. Fischer-Hüllstrung recalled that Bonhoeffer "climbed the stairs to the gallows, brave and composed. . . . In the almost fifty years that I have worked as a doctor, I have hardly ever seen a man die so entirely submissive to the will of God." [9]

Concerning death itself, Bonhoeffer had written, "Come now, highest of feasts on the way to freedom eternal, Death strike off the fetters, break down the walls that oppress us, our bedazzled soul and our ephemeral body, that we may see at last the sight which here was not vouchsafed us. Freedom, we sought you long in discipline, action, suffering. Now as we die we see you and know you at last, face to face." [10]

It was helpful for me to know the circumstances surrounding Bonhoeffer's execution. He had been asked to conduct a service on Sunday, April 8. After some reluctance he did preach and used the text, "And with his stripes we are healed. . . . By his great mercy we have been born anew to a living hope through the resurrection of Jesus." [11]

At the conclusion of the service two guards entered the chapel and said, "Prisoner Bonhoeffer, get ready to come with us." By means of an English airman who was also in prison, he sent a farewell message to the Bishop of Chichester. "This is the end. For me, the beginning of life." The next day he was hanged.

For Bonhoeffer there were six great decisions.

The first was the decision to be "in Christ." The great theme of his life centered around these words "in Christ." Albert Camus had said, "man is the only creature who refuses to be what he is." It was Bonhoeffer's determination to find answers to the question, "What does it really mean to live in the world of Christ?"

For most of us here this has been the first and most significant of the major decisions of our lives. As he made these decisions he held before himself the following faith. "Behind all the slogans and catchwords of ecclesiastical controversy, necessary though they are, there arises a more determined quest for him who is the sole object of it all, for Jesus Christ himself. What did Jesus mean to say to us? What is his will for us today? How can he help us to be good Christians in the modern world? In the last resort, what we want to know is not, what would this or that man, or this or that church, have of us, but what Jesus Christ himself wants of us." [12]

This commitment to Jesus involved his total personality. In his book *The Cost of Discipleship* he wrote:

"Cheap grace is the preaching of forgiveness without requiring repentance, baptism without church discipline, communion without confession, absolution without personal confession. Cheap grace is grace without discipleship, grace without the cross, grace without Jesus Christ, living and incarnate. Costly grace is the treasure hidden in the field; for the sake of it a man will gladly go and sell all that he has. It is the pearl of great price to buy for which the merchant will sell all his goods. It is the kingly rule of Christ, for whose sake a man will pluck out the eye which causes him to stumble, it is the call of Jesus Christ at which the disciple leaves his nets and follows him. Costly grace is the gospel which must be sought again and again, the gift which must be asked for, the door at which a man must knock. Such grace is costly because it calls us to him to follow Jesus Christ. It is costly because it costs a man his life, and it is grace because it gives a man the only true life." [13]

The second major decision was for the Confessional church. It was his belief that "The church is Christ's presence in the world." He felt that man must make a choice between the true church and the syncretist church—between the word of God and the word of God watered down by pagan ideology.

So strong was his feeling that the call was to the Confessional church rather than the German church, that he said, "Anyone who deliberately disassociated himself from the Confessional Church cuts himself off from salvation." [14]

This decision has been similar to the decision that many of us have made in this country. I was reared a true son of the deep South. Early in my ministry I had to make the decision of whether or not I would be "Southern-Christian" or a Christian. Would I be part of a church that would say that the conditions for membership were not only acceptance of Jesus Christ as Lord and Savior but would add to this requirement that a man had to be white?

Many men have left the ministry over this issue. I am reminded of the statement of Abraham Lincoln to the effect that he would join any church that made the basis of its membership and its creed nothing more or less than the two great commandments that we should love God with all our heart and our neighbor as ourselves.

If you think that this is a problem only in Germany, you should have a talk with some of your minister friends, and you will understand the agony that they and Dietrich Bonhoeffer shared.

The third decision of his life, and one that was equally unpopular, was the decision to throw in his lot with the ecumenical movement. The German people looked upon this as a form of Christian internationalism that stood in opposition to their glorification of the Fatherland. It was difficult in those days, as it is now, to be an internationalist, but Bonhoeffer felt that if he shot a man who was a Christian, he could be shooting Jesus Christ, for any man in Christ was Christ in the world.

He could not set being a German above being a Christian.

Again many of us have faced the same issue. Where there is conflict between the current idolatry of America and the attitude that if America does it, it is right, many of us have had to take a stand that our only Lord is Jesus, the son of God, and that we must choose between obeying him and Caesar.

This is not a cheap internationalism, or a sentimentality, but a deep personal conviction that we have a loyalty to Jesus Christ that is above our loyalty to family, state, nation, race, or our heritage.

The other morning I attended a meeting of the Rotary group. During the meeting one of the men made a speech in which he said that Rotary, as represented by the downtown Dallas Rotary Club, represented the hope of brotherhood in our world.

After the speech I asked him if he really believed this, and he affirmed that it was true. I then remarked that ping-pong players from all over the world could get together and happily discuss ping-pong—and that Rotarians from all over the world could get together and discuss their business interests—but that as a member of one of the largest Rotary clubs in the world, he did not seem to me to be making sense. One of the great problems of our world is race, and the Dallas Rotary group, with over five hundred members within a city that is 20 percent black, does not have in its membership a single black man. The Rotary fellowship is a fellowship of those of like economic and social interests. As long as they are discussing those interests, they can be brothers. The church of Jesus Christ is comprised of those who have committed themselves only to Christ. This cuts across the generation gap, the racial divisions, the gaps of economy and sex and unites us all in one in him.

The fourth decision was to take up political action against the Nazi administration and to plot the death of Adolph Hitler.

As Bonhoeffer said, "Christians in Germany will face the terrible alternative of either willing the defeat of their nation in order that Christian civilization may survive, or willing the victory of their nation and thereby destroying our civilization. I know which of these alternatives I must choose, but I cannot make that choice in security." [15]

It was in this context that he also discussed the matter of his own personal innocence as related to the guilt that would be incurred should he be part of killing another man. He came to the conclusion that personal innocence was not as important as his "responsibility for men."

The fifth decision was for marriage. At the time of his death he was engaged to Maria von Wedemeyer.

For many of us the decision to marry is a natural one. With him it was more difficult because of his commitments. After he had made the decision he wrote this, "What a blessing it is, in such distressing times, to belong to a large closely knit family, where each trusts the other and stands by him. When pastors were arrested, I sometimes used to think that it must be easiest for those of them who were unmarried. But I did not know then what the warmth that radiates from the love of a wife and family can mean in the cold air of imprisonment, and how in just such times of separation the feeling of belonging together through thick and thin actually grows stronger." [16]

One of the most beautiful descriptions of marriage that I have ever read is his statement, "Marriage is more than your love for each other. It has a higher dignity and power, for it is God's holy ordinance, through which he wills to perpetuate the human race till the end of time. In your love you see only your two selves in the world, but in marriage you are a link in the chain of the generations, which God causes to come and to pass away to his glory, and calls into his kingdom. In your love you see only the heaven of your happiness, but in marriage you are placed at a post of responsibility toward the world and mankind. Your love is your own private possession, but marriage is more than something personal—it is a status, an office. Just as it is the crown, and not merely your love for each other that keeps you together in the sight of God and man . . . It is not your love that sustains the marriage, but from now on, the marriage that sustains your love." [17]

It was in jail that he made his final decision. It was a rather simple one for him. It was the decision to use most profitably his periods of loneliness and suffering. He became a source of inspiration and joy to the other prisoners. One fellow-prisoner said of him, "He was always in good spirits, and invariably kind and considerate to everyone—so much so that, to my surprise, even his guards soon fell under his spell. In our relationship it was always he who remained hopeful, while I sometimes suffered from depression. He never tired of repeating that only that fight is lost in which you admit defeat. How often did he smuggle a scrap of paper into my hands on which he had written words of comfort and faith from the Bible! He was also optimistic regarding his own situation." [18]

The faith that kept him going was expressed in another paragraph that he wrote, "I believe that God can and will bring good out of evil, even out of the greatest evil. For that purpose he needs men who make the best use of everything. I believe that God will give us all the strength we need to help us to resist in all times of distress. But he never gives it in advance, lest we should rely on ourselves and not on him alone. A faith such as this should allay all our fears for the future. I believe that even our mistakes and shortcomings are turned to good account, and that it is no harder for God to deal with them than with our supposedly good deeds. I believe that God is no timeless fate, but that he waits for and answers sincere prayers and responsible actions." [19]

Perhaps the man's attitude is more clearly expressed by words he frequently used to his fellow-prisoners when he said, "The only fight which is lost is that which we give up."

# John F. Kennedy

# In Memoriam

*This chapter is a sermon printed word for word as it was preached in First Presbyterian Church in Dallas on Sunday morning, November 24, 1963, after President Kennedy was shot in Dallas on Friday, November 22, 1963.*

*The First Presbyterian Church, Dallas is about three hundred yards from the city jail. Just prior to preaching the sermon, I was informed that we had just been cut off the air, and that Lee Harvey Oswald had been shot in the basement of the jail. The whole area was surrounded by police, and I was told that the congregation was not to leave except as the police approved.*

*The shock of knowing that Oswald had just been shot, and that we could not tell the congregation until the end of the service, had a profound effect upon me as I delivered this sermon.* TAF

As we of Dallas seek to compose ourselves after the assassination of President Kennedy, I imagine that all have similar feelings.

At first I felt horror that our president had been assassinated. Then there was a wave of humiliation that it happened in our city. These feelings are giving way now to sympathy for the families that have been bereaved, disquietude about our city, uncertainty about the future.

Amid these emotions I keep asking myself whether or not there is a word from God in our situation—a word of comfort for a bereaved family, a word to help us understand what has happened in our midst and prevent its ever happening again, a word about the future of our nation.

First of all, I would want to send a message of sympathy to the bereaved family. Under the circumstances, this is the least that we of Dallas could do.

During the past few months the Kennedy family has had more than their share of trouble. All of us are proud of Mrs. Kennedy. Through this great tragedy she has acted the part of a magnificent first lady. The fact that her husband was president of the United States does not lessen her loss and grief. It only adds new dimensions to her distress.

We also recognize that in addition to grief there is the temptation to bitterness—a bitterness directed to those fanners of hatred who have made President Kennedy the target of their most vitriolic and poisonous accusations.

What message of consolation can we send to the families? We can remind them of the words of 1 Corinthians 15: 58, "Therefore, my beloved brethren, be steadfast, immovable, always abounding in the work of the Lord, knowing that in the Lord your labor is not in vain."

To begin with we can tell them that there are certain memories that can be sources of joy and pride and therefore of comfort. They can recall his meteoric rise from the halls of Congress to the highest office in the world, the presidency of the United States—and that, before he was forty-four years old. Such memories can serve as a challenge to meet and overcome their own difficulties.

They can also recall the high idealism of this man. His dream of brotherhood and peace can inspire them to seek the strength to live above their hatreds and find the answers to their bitterness.

They can remember his desire to be of service to his country, no matter what the cost. During the war he did not seek assignments that were easy or safe. In a war where the chances were one in fifty of being killed, he sought the danger spots. This same courage and dedication led him to seek the office of president, knowing that among former presidents of the United States one out of twelve had been assassinated.

The family can find courage in the legacy of courage he left them—forgiveness in the example of brotherhood he worked to achieve—desire to overcome in the heritage of ambition that has been bequeathed to them.

The family can also find comfort in the knowledge that through his death he may well achieve a place in history alongside our greatest men; and at the same time, may possibly accomplish in death what might have been denied him in life.

Men who die normal deaths are remembered by their accomplishments. Men who die the death of a martyr are remembered by their ideals. Few of us today remember that Lincoln failed miserably in the leadership of his cabinet, in his control of Congress, and in his ability to find adequate military leadership. Because of his assassination, the world has forgotten his failures and recalls only his ideals.

It may well be that the same thing will be true of John F. Kennedy. All of us shared his dreams of a strong America, of ample and equal opportunity for all, of peace among the nations of the earth, of brotherhood and justice among men. His death may make him a martyr to these great causes and so a national hero.

The family would do well to take note of another fact of American history. Our people do not allow a true martyr to die in vain. It may take time, but the American people have always arisen to follow the ideals of their martyrs. From Valley Forge, through Gettysburg, to the fall of Corregidor, we have not allowed the dead to die in vain. The noble ideals for which he fought may have a better chance of becoming a reality through his death than through his life. The Commander of the P.T. 109, who would gladly have given his life to aid in a military victory, may now at last have given his life to make real those things of peace, brotherhood, justice, and opportunity for which he fought and lived.

There are yet other comforts for the bereaved. Nearly three thousand years ago one man who had been the leader of his nation wrote of his own experience, saying, "Though I walk through the valley of the shadow of death, I will fear no evil, for Thou art with me." He, or someone like him, also wrote, "God is our refuge and strength, a very present help in trouble." I have found, and can commend to the bereaved families the knowledge that God will be present and supportive. The man whom Protestants and Roman Catholics alike worship as God and Savior has said, "Lo, I am with you always, even unto the end of the world." He has proved that promise in many of our lives.

To a family that professes the Christian faith, there is one
other word of comfort and hope. Our Savior has said, "Let not
your hearts be troubled; believe in God, believe also in Me. In
my Father's house are many rooms. . . ." [1] "I am the resurrection and the life; he that believes in me, though he die, yet shall
he live." [2]

I am sure that President Kennedy would not like the Heaven
that many aspire to. They feel that Heaven is a place where we
shall rest an eon or two, and then take a nap after lunch and
supper. This man of ambition and vigor would be bored to tears
by such indolence. Heavenly rest would not be very Heavenly.
We worship a God who works. Jesus said, "My father works, and
I work." We consider Heaven as a promotion similar to moving
from the mayorship of a small hamlet to the presidency of the
United States. The new opportunities and new responsibilities
will be such a thrill that the things left behind will soon be
forgotten. To say that death is a personal tragedy for one so
young, for one at the pinnacle of responsibility is to indicate a
lack of understanding of the Christian interpretation of death.

For myself and for our city I would like very much to say
these things to the family. It might help stanch the flow of grief
from their broken hearts.

It is relatively easy for me to say words of sympathy and
comfort to the bereaved family. But a black pall has been spread
over our city. We have been a proud town. We gloried in being
called "Big D."

But something has happened. As in the case of a cancer, it is
difficult to tell its time of birth, or its exact areas of growth, but
we know it is here. It has developed as we have allowed the
apostles of religious bigotry and the peddlers of political pornog-
raphy to excite to uncontrolled lust the weak-minded and emotionally unbalanced of our town. We allowed them to continue
their dirty work, because they supported our conservative
churches and our conservative political candidates.

Increasingly we became aware that something disturbing was
developing in our city. It erupted here and there until the world
started taking note of our changing image. It finally got so bad
that our president was advised not to come to Dallas.

All of us wanted him to come. Many who disagreed with him
stood on the streets to wave welcome to him, feeling that we

should redeem the image of a hostile and uncontrolled town. We wanted to prove to the world once again that we were a gracious, generous, and free city. We were "Big D."

Now the president is dead. Dead of an assassin's bullet fired in "Big D."

The first few hours after the assassination were the most horrible in my life. If President Kennedy had died of a heart attack, it would not have been near so tragic. If he had been assassinated in Washington, our grief would have been far less than the torment we felt during those early hours. Our consciences were getting hold of us. We knew that we had played with fire! Now the house had burned down! The sky was black with our chickens coming home to roost.

After a few hours we found that it was not one of our own right-wing extremists. He was an extremist of the left, reared in a neighboring town. We felt some better. We had had a reprieve. While we shared the corporate guilt of our nation, it was not the personal guilt of having allowed the demonic element of our city to run wild and encourage them in their indecent activities.

For a few hours we had faced ourselves. For an instant we saw that lies are lies, even though they are politically motivated; that rumor can excite the ignorant; that half-truths can inflame the emotionally sick. Those hours may have brought us to true repentance. Our future actions will tell whether or not this is so.

From this day on, any man who hints the president is a Communist and will not prove it in court, who distributes literature calling him an adulterer and can do no more than produce a picture of him in front of someone's home, who says that the president is deliberately destroying the Constitution and will not give his Congressmen ample evidence of his treason should find no place on our platforms, no newspapers to give him publicity, no acceptance in our society.

I pray to God that we have learned our lesson. Only fools say that lightning does not strike twice in the same place.

There is a second lesson that we in Dallas should have learned. The alleged assassin worked in a building where there were scores of Christians. Had no one of them talked to him about Jesus Christ? He had a room in a rooming house in our city. Did none of the roomers or the landlady think to talk to him about a Savior? He lived in one of our church saturated

suburbs. Did no one urge him to attend Sunday school? He
was educated in the schools of a neighboring town. Did none
of the young people think him worth working on for their faith,
their group, or their church?

We have lived under the false assumption that other people's
religion is their own business. We have not wanted to interfere
in such a personal matter. But now our president is dead! We
realize that a person's religion is society's business when someone
shoots the president, or when a drunken man kills our child with
his car.

Those who are indifferent to the expanded program of the
church should think deeply over these implications.

It is a matter of irony that I have talked twice recently with
our governor about trying to do something about the ethical
problem of children reared in religionless schools. He now lies
in a Dallas hospital, victim of a man who has never known God.
He has been waiting for me, and others like me, to try to point
a way out of our problem.

I would say one other word to our city. During his term as
vice-president, Harry Truman was called one day and asked to
come to the White House. He was met by Mrs. Roosevelt, who
told him that her husband had been stricken and was dead. We
are told that Mr. Truman broke down in tears. After he had
regained his composure, he said, "Is there anything I can do for
you?" Her reply was, "That is not the issue. Is there anything
I can do for you?"

We may, or may not, support the policies of Lyndon Baines
Johnson; but no man deserves the treatment that has been given
to John F. Kennedy. While holding to our convictions, we can
support the office of the president of the United States, and in
complete sincerity ask of our new president, "Is there anything
we can do for you?"

There are words of God for the family. Those words in 1
Corinthians 15:58, "Therefore, my beloved brethren, be steadfast, immovable, always abounding in the work of the Lord,
knowing that in the Lord your labor is not in vain." There are
also other words, "God is our refuge and strength, a very present help in trouble." Then there are expressions of hope, "Let
not your hearts be troubled; believe in God, believe also in Me.
In my father's house are many rooms. . . ." These can strength-
en and sustain a Christian family in bereavement.

The word to our city must be different. "Except ye repent, ye shall likewise perish."

What is the word to our nation? Two texts speak to my heart at this hour. The first from Proverbs 14:34, "Righteousness exalts a nation, but sin is a reproach to any people." The second is from Romans 8:28, "We know that in everything God works for good with those who love him. . . ." These two texts say the same thing. The righteous and those who love God are equivalent in scriptural interpretation. God works in everything for good to those who love him and seek to maintain a right relationship with him.

Other nations have been noted for strong men. But we have not been noted for strong figures in the sense that Hitler and Stalin were strong. We have been noted for men of ideals—for leaders of character—for a citizenry that expects character and integrity in its leadership.

The future of our nation will depend far more upon the character of the American people and what we expect of our president than upon what he intends or tries to do. In the ultimate sense, the president is a slave of the people. If we expect justice, brotherhood, character, and integrity, our political leadership will give these to us. If we expect them to take bribes, to live off corruption, to ignore the needs of the people, they will be our servants in this also.

We cannot say why God has allowed this to happen, but we do know:

> Though the cause of evil prosper,
> Yet 'tis truth alone is strong;
> Though her portion be the scaffold,
> And upon the throne be wrong,
> Yet that scaffold sways the future,
> And behind the dim unknown,
> Standeth God within the shadows
> Keeping watch upon his own.[3]

As long as we are a nation committed to the Lord, I have no fear for the future. Until we will commit our ways unto him, I have no hope for the future.

As far as our nation is concerned I would pray:

> God bless our native land;
> Firm may she ever stand

Through storm and night:
When the wild tempests rave,
Ruler of wind and wave,
Do Thou our country save
    By Thy great might.

For her our prayer shall rise
To God above the skies;
    On Him we wait;
Thou who art ever nigh,
Guarding with watchful eye,
To thee aloud we cry,
    God save the State.

Nor for this land alone,
But be God's mercies shown
    From shore to shore;
And may the nations see
That men should brothers be
And form one family
    The wide world o'er.[4]

# Martin Luther King, Jr.

# I Have a Dream

ARNOLD TOYNBEE, writing almost half a century ago, may have been prophetic in his estimate of the Negro's participation in American life and his influence upon the Christian faith. He said:

"The Negro appears to be answering our tremendous challenge with a religious response which may prove in the event, when it can be seen in retrospect, to bear comparison with the ancient Oriental's response to the challenge from his Roman masters. The Negro has not, indeed, brought any ancestral religion of his own from Africa to captivate the hearts of his White fellow-citizens in America. His primitive social heritage was of so frail a texture that, save for a few shreds, it was scattered to the winds on the impact of our Western Civilization. Thus he came to America spiritually as well as physically naked; and he had met the emergency by covering his nakedness with his enslaver's cast-off clothes. The Negro has adapted himself to his new social environment by rediscovering in Christianity certain original meanings and values which Western Christendom has long ignored. Opening a simple and impressionable mind to the Gospels, he has discovered that Jesus was a prophet who came into the world not to confirm the mighty in their seats but to exalt the humble and meek. The Syrian slave immigrants who once brought Christianity into Roman Italy performed the miracle of establishing a new religion which was alive in the place of an old religion which was already dead. It is possible that the Negro slave immigrants who have found Christianity in America may perform the greater miracle of raising the dead to life. With their childlike spiritual intuition and their genius for giving

spontaneous aesthetic expression to emotional religious experience, they may perhaps be capable of kindling the cold grey
ashes of Christianity which have been transmitted to them by us
until, in their hearts, the divine fire glows again. It is thus perhaps, if at all, that Christianity may conceivably become the
living faith of a dying civilization for the second time. If this
miracle were indeed to be performed by an American Negro
Church, that would be the most dynamic response to the challenge of social penalization that had yet been made by man." [1]

The fulfillment of these words is exemplified in the life and
work of Martin Luther King, Jr. He was born January 15, 1929,
son of a Baptist minister. After graduating from Morehouse College in 1948, he attended Crozier Theological Seminary. He received his Ph.D. from Boston University in 1955. From 1954 to
1959 he was pastor of the Dexter Avenue Baptist Church in
Montgomery, and from 1959 until his death was copastor with
his father at the Ebenezer Baptist Church in Atlanta. He rose
to nationwide fame in 1956 when he was in charge of the city-
wide boycott of Montgomery public transportation facilities by
Negroes reacting against Jim Crow practices. He was the leading
force in the wave of restaurant and lunch counter sit-ins in 1960
and the drive to open all public accommodations shortly thereafter. He reached the pinnacle of his public acclaim with his
march on Washington, August 28, 1963, delivering his famous "I
Have a Dream" address.

The rise of younger, more militant black leaders, whose theme
was black power rather than a matter of faith, brought Martin
Luther King into decline in his leadership with the black people.
While he supported black movements, he could not give whole-
hearted endorsement to the more radical groups.

In 1964 he won the Nobel Peace Prize. It is said that more
than any other man he was responsible for the enactment of the
1964 and 1965 civil rights acts. On April 4, 1968, he was shot in
Memphis, Tennessee, less than twenty-four hours after having
delivered one of the most moving addresses of his career.

King was a preacher. It was said of Dietrich Bonhoeffer that
he was the least schizophrenic of the men of his time. The biog-
raphers of Bonhoeffer meant that his life and his words formed

one single unity. This was also true of Martin Luther King, Jr. He did not preach love on Sundays only to practice violence Monday afternoon.

We frequently ask, what makes a man like King tick? What are the inner forces that push him on?

In the great sermon he preached the night before he was assassinated, King discusses the parable of the good Samaritan. Having talked about the dangers of the "bloody road" from Jerusalem to Jericho, he tells how the priest and the Levite might very well have asked, "If I stop to help this man, what will happen to me?" It was entirely possible that the robbers were still hiding, waiting to pounce on another victim, or that the man himself might be faking and be a part of the ambush scheme. King goes on to say that the real issue for the Samaritan was not, "If I stop to help this man, what will happen to me?" but rather, "If I do not stop to help this man, what will happen to him?"

It was this kind of thinking that took King to Memphis on his last trip. He felt that if he did not go to Memphis to help the garbage workers, they would be more likely to continue in their deprived condition without improvement. It was this same type of thinking that motivated his other drives.

Some have suggested that men like King have a messianic complex. Such statements have been made about Woodrow Wilson, Winston Churchill, Charles DeGaulle, Franklin Roosevelt. It seems to me that we have to recognize the difference between ambition and ability. Both Churchill and DeGaulle were absolutely confident that they had the information and the ability necessary to lead their people to victory and greatness. Acting on their beliefs, both of them succeeded. In exactly the same way, a football or a basketball team must have belief in themselves, based upon the reality of past experience, if they are to have success.

To deny one's abilities in false humility is a hypocrisy even greater than asserting abilities one does not have. For the genius to aspire to nothing more than an assembly-line job is a greater sin than for the assembly-line man to aspire to be a genius.

King recognized that he had charismatic gifts, and that only

as he used those gifts would his people find the freedom that he
believed was guaranteed them by the Declaration of Independence and that was made obligatory by our Christian faith.

King was always conscious of impending death. In the speech
the night before his assassination, he talked of his plane having
been delayed in Atlanta that morning because of the extra pre-
cautions that the airline had to take, both in protecting the plane
and its passengers. He mentioned the threats to his life that had
come from his "sick white brothers," even after he had arrived
in Memphis.

He wanted to live. Living was exciting, adventuresome, satisfy-
ing. He told of a letter that he had received following an earlier
assassination attempt. He had been autographing books in a New
York store. A black woman came up and stabbed him in the chest
with a knife. It was reported the next morning in the *New York
Times* that the point of the knife was poised against the aorta,
and that if he had just sneezed, the pressure generated would
have been enough to have punctured the aorta, and he would
have drowned in his own blood. During his hospitalization he
received letters and telegrams, including ones from the president
of the United States, the vice president, and the governor of
New York, but he had one letter from a ninth grade student
in White Plains, New York, which impressed him more than any
other. She wrote simply, "I am so happy that you didn't sneeze."

He says that he was glad he did not sneeze, because if he had
sneezed he would not have lived to see the sit-ins and the victories that they won in opening restaurants and lunch counters
to blacks. If he had sneezed, he would not have lived to participate in the movement to open public accommodations to blacks.
If he had sneezed, he would not have been able to participate in
the march on Washington where he spoke of his great dream.

Following this, he says that what happened to him from that
time on did not really matter, because, as he said, he had been to
the mountaintop. He had seen the Promised Land. He did not
know whether he was going to be able to move into the Promised
Land with his people, but he knew that they were going to get
there. His death did not concern him, because he knew that he
and his people would be free at last.

His belief in life beyond the grave was expressed in great

beauty when he said that death was not a period at the end of the sentence of life, but was a comma. Life continues on beyond death. In his preaching he told the church that it must continue to hold out hope to its people—young and old—for life and for fellowship, joy, freedom, and useful service beyond the grave.

Life was exciting. Death was a comma, and the future always lay before him.

Basic to King's program was his belief in nonviolence. In this he was a follower of Jesus and Gandhi. When King organized the Southern Christian Leadership Conference, they developed disciplined exercises in nonviolent resistance. They practiced their responses to slaps in the face, being hissed at and spat upon, being hit with billyclubs, hosed with water, kicked in the groin.

He believed that retaliation produced retaliation, and that we could not continue our society with its wars, its riots in the city, its fire bombs and its snipers. He believed in nonviolence for all people.

He also believed that nonviolence produced creative results. He felt that nonviolence on the part of the blacks would appeal to the conscience of the whites.

"I am still convinced that the philosophy and practice of nonviolence affords a more excellent way to improve the inadequacies existing in the American social system. The method of nonviolent resistance is effective and it has a way of disarming the opponent. It exposes his moral defenses. It weakens his morale. And at the same time it works on his conscience. I believe we will win it, because the goal of America is freedom. Abused and scorned though we be, our destiny is tied up with the destiny of America." [2]

As I indicated above, he did not feel that we would be any better off if we had tyranny imposed by the blacks rather than tyranny imposed by the whites. In one of his great statements recorded at the Mt. Zion Baptist Church in Cincinnati, Ohio, he said:

"More than anything else we have to learn to love. In America the white man must love the black man, and the black man must love the white man, because we are all tied together in a single garment of destiny, and we can't keep having riots every summer in our cities. We can't keep having all these problems in our nation. . . . Now in our responding to the oppression and the hatred that we face, we must not turn around and do the same thing. You see, you never solve one problem of tyranny by substituting a new problem or a new tyranny. The doctrine of black supremacy is as evil as the doctrine of white supremacy. God is not interested in the freedom of black men and brown men and yellow men, but God is interested in the freedom of the whole human race . . . the creation of a society where all men will live together as brothers, and every man will respect the dignity and the worth of human personality. And the one way that every man will be able to do this is to remember that one word that Jesus talked about so often—that is the word 'love.' " [3]

King seemed to feel that America was the one country where all people could be free. I shall let King speak to you through his eloquent words:

"I have a dream that one day this nation will rise up—live out the true meaning of its creed that 'we hold those truths to be self-evident that all men are created equal.'

"I have a dream that one day on the red hills of Georgia the sons of former slaves and the sons of former slaveowners will be able to sit down together at the table of brotherhood.

"I have a dream that one day even the state of Mississippi; a desert state sweltering with the heat of injustice and oppression, will be transformed into an oasis of freedom and justice. . . .

"I have a dream that one day every valley shall be exalted, every hill and mountain shall be made low, and rough places will be made plains, and the crooked places will be made straight, and the glory of the Lord shall be revealed, and all flesh shall see it together.

"This is our hope. This is the faith with which I return to the South. With this faith we will be able to hew out of the mountain of despair a stone of hope. With this faith we will be able to transform the jangling discords of our nation into a beautiful symphony of brotherhood. With this faith we will be able to work together, to pray together, to struggle together, to go to jail together, to stand up for freedom together, knowing that we will be free one day.

"This will be the day when all of God's children will be able to sing with a new meaning,

> My country 'tis of thee,
> sweet land of liberty.
> Of thee I sing.
> Land where my fathers died,
> Land of the pilgrims' pride
> From every mountainside
> Let freedom ring.[4]

"I love this country too much to see it drift as it has. God did not call America to do what she is doing in the world now. God did not call America to engage in a senseless, unjust war, as the war in Vietnam is. We are criminals in that war. We have committed more war crimes than almost any nation in the world." [5]

It should be noted in all of his speeches that he was not yet ready to give up on America. This faith in his country and its dream did not keep him from seeing the weaknesses of America. Without withholding criticism he supported his nation as few other black leaders have done in the past two decades.

It is my wish that America could be as great as he dreamed it would be. In his sermon "The Drum Major Instinct" he points out that the desire for leadership on the part of the apostles, James and John, was an honorable desire. Every man should desire to sit on the right and left hand of his Lord. But the places of honor are to be reserved for those who are the servants of the people, rather than the masters, and he calls upon America to be the servant of humanity.

King was born into a minister's family, made an early decision to enter the ministry himself, was trained as a theologian, and was pastor of a church all during his professional life. While the institutional church disturbed him, he supported it with all of his life. He believed in its Savior. He honored its ideals. He worked within its organization.

This is not to say that he withheld criticism of the church. Once speaking in Westminster Abbey he called to mind that

this great cathedral had been the center for religious worship
for the British during that period when they controlled one-
third of the world in their colonial empire, and that the Westminster Abbey and the Church of England it represented had
never raised its voice against the evils of colonialism. As others
who have visited the great cathedrals of Europe are aware, the
cathedrals built to the glory of God throughout that vast con-
tinent now stand empty as the judgment of God upon the church
preaching in such a way as to be irrelevant to the needs of
people.

His sharpest scorn was at times saved for the white pulpit. In
his letter from the Birmingham jail he said to his white clergymen friends:

"I must make two honest confessions to you, my Christian and
Jewish brothers. First, I must confess that over the past few
years I have been gravely disappointed with the white moderate.
I have almost reached the regrettable conclusion that the Negro's
great stumbling block in his stride toward freedom is not the
White Citizen's Counciler or the Ku Klux Klanner but the white
moderate who is more devoted to 'order' than to justice; who
prefers a negative peace which is the absence of tension to a
positive peace which is the presence of justice; who constantly
says 'I agree with you in the goal you seek, but I cannot agree
with your methods'; who paternalistically believes he can set
the timetable for another man's freedom; who lives by a mythical
concept of time and who constantly advises the Negro to wait
for a 'more convenient season'. Shallow understanding from people of good will is more frustrating than absolute misunderstand-
ing from people of ill will. Lukewarm acceptance is much more
bewildering than outright rejection." 6

To those who have said "wait," he replies:

"For years now I have heard the word 'Wait.' It rings in the
ear of every Negro with piercing familiarity. This 'Wait' has
almost always meant 'Never.' As one of our distinguished jurists
once said, 'justice too long delayed is justice denied!' " 7

He also had a word for the black church. When he spoke of
the pitfalls before the white church he was inclined to speak in

terms of "they," but when observing the black church, he could speak of "we."

He pointed to the two tendencies of the black church that could lead to its downfall. He said there were black churches that would freeze people out, and there were black churches that would burn people up.

The group that would freeze people out was led by ministers and laity that were ashamed of their black background, and like many modern Jews wanted to forget their distinctiveness. In their sermons their preachers delivered well-prepared sermons on theological subjects, but dealt with none of the relevant issues of life. The membership of these black churches was made up of doctors, lawyers, school teachers, and the like.

King said that they would talk of their membership rolls in such a way as to make it appear that only those who had the education really counted. Thus they were separating themselves from people—from the common blacks and their needs.

The other weakness—the churches that would burn people up—was that they would become emotional churches "with more religion in their hands and feet than in their hearts and souls." They would have a great emotional experience in church, but one that produced nothing in terms of a change in character or a change in society.

To the black and white churches alike he pointed to God's statement that what He required was not just intelligence or emotion, but a reaction of the will where people would do justice, love mercy, and walk humbly with their God.

In a magnificent sermon, "A Knock at Midnight," he pointed out that people still looked to the church for the bread of life. When they come at inopportune hours, seeking that bread, it is the responsibility of the church to have it available for the spiritually hungry.

The bread of which he spoke was the bread of hope which should be offered to the aged, the sick, and the dying—a bread that freed them from the fears and frailties of this life. The church should keep fresh the bread of salvation which would offer to the guilt-ridden young man and young woman some answer other than the answer of alcohol, drugs, and sex, and remind them that "there is a fountain filled with blood, flowing from Emmanuel's veins."

The church was to offer the bread of life wherein people would find acceptance, even though they were sinful, and a unity of fellowship that transcended race and class to where an individual would be respected for what he was inside himself, rather than for the color of his skin or the source of his national origin.

And so he called upon the church to offer to the world the bread of life which had been entrusted to it.

King sought to be this kind of pastor and preacher, and those who heard his sermons were invariably pointed beyond King to Him who came that men might have life and have it abundantly.

To you we would affirm that along with Dietrich Bonhoeffer, King was the least schizophrenic of men. There was no division between his public words and his public action. He did create tensions within our society, but they were never tensions just for the sake of tensions. As he wrote in his letter from the Birmingham jail, "Non-violent direction action seeks to foster such a tension that a community which has constantly refused to negotiate is forced to confront the issue."

In closing I would remind you of one of the most significant paragraphs that King ever uttered. Each one of us should hang it over the door of our minds, and perhaps over the doors of our offices and our homes. "Every man should have something he would be willing to die for. A man who won't die for something is not really fit to live."

# NOTES

## Chapter 1 — Thomas More

1. Desmond Morris, *The Naked Ape* (New York: McGraw-Hill Book Co., 1967), p. 125.

## Chapter 2 — George Washington

1. *American Heritage* 20, no. 4, p. 76.
2. Frederic Fox, "Pater Patriae as Pater Familias," *American Heritage* 14, no. 3, p. 33.
3. Ibid.
4. Ibid., pp. 36–37.
5. Ibid., p. 33.
6. Edmund Fuller and David E. Green, *God in the White House* (New York: Crown Publishers, Inc., 1968), p. 15.
7. Ibid.
8. Ibid., p. 16.
9. *Harvard Classics*, 43:242–43.
10. Fuller and Green, p. 16.
11. Cornel Adam Lengyel, *Presidents of the United States* (New York: Bantam Books, Inc., 1961), p. 14.

## Chapter 3 — John Adams

1. Edmund Fuller and David E. Green, *God in the White House* (New York: Crown Publishers, Inc., 1968), p. 25.
2. Ibid.
3. Irving Stone, *Those Who Love* (New York: Doubleday & Co., Inc., 1965), p. 59.
4. Cornel Adam Lengyel, *Presidents of the United States* (New York: Bantam Books, Inc., 1961), p. 16.
5. *The Growing Years, The Life History of the United States* (New York: Time, Inc., 1963), 3:34.
6. Fuller and Green, p. 23.
7. *Encyclopaedia Britannica*, 1:147.
8. Fuller and Green, p. 24.
9. *The Growing Years*, 3:36.
10. Ibid., 3:37.
11. Lengyel, p. 16.
12. Fuller and Green, p. 27.
13. Ibid., p. 26.
14. Lengyel, p. 16.

## Chapter 4 — Thomas Jefferson

1. Edmund Fuller and David E. Green, *God in the White House* (New York: Crown Publishers, Inc., 1968), p. 38.
2. Cornel Adam Lengyel, *Presidents of the United States* (New York: Bantam Books, Inc., 1961), p. 19.
3. Thomas Fleming, *The Man from Monticello* (New York: William Morrow & Co., Inc., 1969), p. 281.

4. Fuller and Green, p. 30.
5. Ibid., p. 35.
6. *Encyclopaedia Britannica*, p. 988.
7. Fuller and Green, p. 35.
8. Fleming, p. 337.
9. Ibid., p. 277.
10. Ibid., p. 367.
11. Ibid., p. 368.
12. Lengyel, p. 17.
13. Josiah Holland, "The Day's Demand."

## Chapter 5 — *John Quincy Adams*

1. *American Heritage* 12, no. 3, p. 65.
2. Ibid.
3. Ibid., p. 71.
4. Edmund Fuller and David E. Green, *God in the White House* (New York: Crown Publishers, Inc., 1968), p. 54.
5. Ibid., p. 57.
6. Ibid., p. 58.
7. John F. Kennedy, *Profiles in Courage* (New York: Harper & Row, Publishers, Inc., 1961), p. 28.
8. Ibid., p. 53.
9. Fuller and Green, p. 58.
10. Ibid., p. 55.
11. Ibid., p. 59.
12. Ibid., pp. 56–57.
13. Kennedy, p. 41.
14. Ibid., p. 71.

## Chapter 7 — *Woodrow Wilson*

1. Josephus Daniels, *The Life of Woodrow Wilson* (New York: Reprint House International, 1924), p. 358.
2. *American Heritage*, August 1956, p. 24.
3. Ibid.
4. *American Heritage,* 1962, p. 30.
5. Ibid., p. 31.
6. Ibid.
7. Ibid., p. 69.
8. Ibid.
9. *American Heritage,* August 1956, p. 26.
10. Ernest R. Mays, *The Progressive Era, The Life History of the United States* (New York: Time, Inc., 1963), 9:101.
11. Daniels, 332.
12. Ibid., p. 330.
13. Ibid., pp. 351–53.
14. Ibid., p. 359.
15. Ibid.

## Chapter 8 — *Churchill, Moses, and God*

1. Winston Churchill, *Amid These Storms* (New York: Charles

Scribner's Sons, 1932), pp. 293–94.

Scribner's Sons, 1932), pp. 293–94.
2. Phylis Moir, *I Was Winston Churchill's Private Secretary* (New York: Wilfred Funk, Inc., 1941), p. 183.
3. Virginia Cowles, *Winston Churchill: The Era and the Man* (New York: Grosset & Dunlap, 1953), p. 64.
4. *Reader's Digest,* December 1964, p. 228.
5. Ibid., p. 246.
6. *Reader's Digest,* January 1965, p. 229.
7. Churchill, p. 194.
8. Exodus 32:31–32, RSV.
9. *Reader's Digest,* December 1964, pp. 222–23.
10. Ibid.
11. *Christianity Today,* 29 January 1965, p. 52.
12. 1 Corinthians 13:1–7, RSV.
13. *Reader's Digest,* January 1954, p. 209.
14. Deuteronomy 30:15–20, RSV.
15. Joshua 24:15, RSV.
16. Matthew 16:24–25.
17. Luke 14:26–27, RSV.
18. Matthew 6:33.
19. *Reader's Digest,* December 1964, p. 248.
20. *Reader's Digest,* January 1965, p. 210.
21. Philippians 1:21, RSV.
22. S. Baring-Gould, "Onward Christian Soldiers," 1865.
23. Arthur Cleveland Coxe, "We Are Living, We Are Dwelling," 1840.

*Chapter 9 — Albert Schweitzer*

1. Magnus C. Ratter, *Albert Schweitzer: Life and Message* (Boston: Beacon Press, 1950), p. 80.
2. John Canning, ed., *100 Great Modern Lives* (New York: Hawthorn Books, Inc., 1965), p. 395.
3. "Albert Schweitzer Speaks Out," *World Book Year Book* (Chicago: Field Enterprises, 1964), pp. 135–36.
4. Ratter, pp. 53–54.
5. *World Book Year Book,* p. 142.
6. Ibid., p. 148.
7. Ratter, pp. 174–75.
8. Ibid., p. 62.
9. Ibid., p. 70.
10. Luke 16:19–31, RSV.

*Chapter 10 — Helen Keller*

1. Robert M. Bartlett, *They Dared to Live* (New York: Association Press, 1939), p. 77.
2. Helen Keller, *The Story of My Life* (New York: Doubleday & Co., Inc., 1954), p. 24.
3. Norman Richards, *Helen Keller: People of Destiny* (Chicago: Children's Press, 1939), p. 14.
4. *Consumer Reports,* April 1971, p. 310.
5. Ibid., p. 18.
6. Keller, p. 14.

7. Ibid., pp. 40–41.
8. Richards, p. 75.
9. Ibid., p. 16.

*Chapter 11 — Pope John XXIII*

1. *World Book Year Book* (Chicago: Field Enterprises, 1964), p. 73.
2. John XXIII, *Wit and Wisdom of Good Pope John,* comp. Henri Fesquet (New York: P. J. Kenedy & Sons, 1964), p. 24.
3. John Canning, ed., *100 Great Modern Lives* (New York: Hawthorn Books, Inc., 1965), p. 470.
4. John XXIII, p. 52.
5. Ibid., p. 55.
6. Ibid., p. 82.
7. *World Book Year Book,* p. 274.
8. Norman Richards, *Pope John XXIII: People of Destiny* (Chicago: Children's Press, 1968), p. 72.
9. John XXIII, p. 53.
10. Canning, p. 472.
11. Ibid.
12. John XXIII, p. 104.
13. Ibid., p. 111–12.
14. Ibid., p. 120.
15. Ibid., p. 122.
16. Ibid., p. 125.
17. Ibid., p. 123.
18. John XXIII, *Journal of a Soul* (New York: McGraw-Hill Book Co., 1964), p. 427.
19. Ibid., p. 430.

*Chapter 12 — Richard E. Byrd*

1. *National Geographic,* July 1957, p. 48.
2. *National Geographic,* September 1957, p. 368.
3. *National Geographic,* October 1959, p. 548.
4. Richard E. Byrd, *Alone* (New York: G. P. Putnam & Sons, 1938), p. 31.
5. Ibid., p. 4.
6. Ibid., p. 7.
7. Ibid., p. 8.
8. Ibid., pp. 34–35.
9. Ibid., pp. 79–80.
10. Ibid., p. 85.
11. Ibid., p. 110.
12. Ibid., p. 154.
13. Ibid., pp. 160–62.
14. Ibid., p. 179.
15. Ibid., pp. 135–36.
16. Ibid., p. 178.
17. Ibid., 183.
18. Ibid., p. 189–90.

*Chapter 13 — Ralph McGill*

1. *Atlanta Journal,* 4 February 1969.

2. Ibid.
3. *Atlanta Constitution,* 5 February 1969.
4. Ibid.
5. Ralph McGill, *A Church a School* (Nashville: Abingdon Press, 1959), pp. 9–10.
6. Ibid., p. 30.
7. *Atlanta Constitution,* 5 February 1969.
8. *Newsweek,* 17 February 1969, p. 72.
9. *Atlanta Constitution,* 5 February 1969.

*Chapter 14 — Dag Hammarskjöld*

1. John Canning, ed., *100 Great Modern Lives* (New York: Hawthorn Books, Inc., 1965), p. 606.
2. Henry P. Van Dusen, *Dag Hammarskjöld: The Statesman and His Faith* (New York: Harper & Row, Publishers, 1967), p. 4.
3. Ibid.
4. Ibid., p. 22.
5. Ibid., p. 47.
6. Sten Soderberg, *Hammarskjöld: A Pictorial Biography* (New York: Viking Press, 1962), p. 6.
7. Ibid., p. 9.
8. Canning, p. 611.
9. Edward R. Murrow, *This I Believe,* ed. Raymond Swing (New York: Simon & Schuster, 1952), pp. 66–67.
10. Van Dusen, pp. 46–47.
11. Dag Hammarskjöld, *Markings,* trans. Leif Sjöberg and W. H. Auden (New York: Alfred A. Knopf, 1968), p. 100.
12. Ibid., pp. 159–60.
13. Ibid., pp. 214–15.
14. Ibid., p. 198.
15. Ibid., p. 205.

*Chapter 15 — Dietrich Bonhoeffer*

1. E. H. Robertson, *Dietrich Bonhoeffer* (Richmond, Va.: John Knox Press, 1966), p. 2.
2. Theodore A. Gill, *A Short Life of Dietrich Bonhoeffer* (New York: Macmillan Co., 1971), p. 42.
3. Ibid., p. 343.
4. J. Martin Bailey and Douglas Gilbert, *The Steps of Bonhoeffer: A Pictorial Album* (New York: Macmillan Co., 1969), p. 8.
5. Ibid., p. 13.
6. Ibid.
7. John D. Godsey, *The Theology of Dietrich Bonhoeffer* (Philadelphia: Westminster Press, 1960), p. 198.
8. Bailey and Gilbert, p. 62.
9. Ibid., p. 15.
10. Ibid., p. 91.
11. Ibid., p. 93.
12. Godsey, p. 47.
13. Dietrich Bonhoeffer, *The Cost of Discipleship* (New York: Macmillan Co., 1960), p. 26.
14. Bailey and Gilbert, p. 8.
15. Ibid., p. 58.

16. Ibid., p. 35.
17. Ibid., p. 83.
18. Godsey, p. 201.
19. Bailey and Gilbert, p. 76.

*Chapter 16 — John F. Kennedy*
1. John 14:1-2.
2. John 11:25.
3. James Russell Lowell, "The Present Crisis," 1845.
4. William E. Hickson, trans., "God Bless Our Native Land," 1836.

*Chapter 17 — Martin Luther King, Jr.*
1. Arnold J. Toynbee, *A Study of History,* ed. D. C. Somervell, abr. ed., 2 vols. (New York: Oxford University Press, Inc., 1947), 1:129.
2. Martin Luther King, Jr., "A Knock at Midnight," as recorded by Nashboro Record Co.
3. Ibid.
4. Martin Luther King, Jr., "I Have a Dream," *The Dolphin Book of Speeches,* ed. George W. Hibbitt (Garden City, N.Y.: Doubleday & Co., Inc., 1965), pp. 176-77.
5. Martin Luther King, Jr., "I Have a Dream," as recorded by 20th Century Fox.
6. Letter from Birmingham jail by Martin Luther King, Jr., *The Christian Century,* 12 June 1963.
7. Ibid.